Pierre Bourdieu's
Political Economy of Being

PIERRE BOURDIEU'S POLITICAL ECONOMY OF BEING

GHASSAN HAGE

Duke University Press
Durham and London

2 0 2 5

© 2025 DUKE UNIVERSITY PRESS
All rights reserved

Designed by A. Mattson Gallagher
Typeset in Garamond Premier
by Westchester Publishing Services

Library of Congress Cataloging-in-
Publication Data
Names: Hage, Ghassan, author.
Title: Pierre Bourdieu's political economy of
being / Ghassan Hage.
Description: Durham : Duke University Press,
2025. | Includes bibliographical references
and index.
Identifiers: LCCN 2024060621 (print)
LCCN 2024060622 (ebook)
ISBN 9781478032625 (paperback)
ISBN 9781478029267 (hardcover)
ISBN 9781478061472 (ebook)
Subjects: LCSH: Bourdieu, Pierre, 1930–2002. |
Bourdieu, Pierre, 1930–2002—Political and
social views.
Classification: LCC HM479.B68 H34 2025
(print) | LCC HM479.B68 (ebook) | DDC
301.01—dc23/eng/20250528
LC record available at https://lccn.loc.
gov/2024060621
LC ebook record available at https://lccn.loc.
gov/2024060622

Contents

Preface

It's early 1991, and I am in Paris for my first time as a postdoc at Pierre Bourdieu's Centre de Sociologie Européenne. I am in a room with a couple of other visitors and casual staff. Bourdieu enters the room, and everyone turns to him. He greets everyone and then walks straight to me and says, "You want to have lunch?" He asks no one else. We walk Rue du Cardinal Lemoine together heading from the Collège de France toward the river. I am internally, and perhaps not so internally, glowing: "Wow, I am walking the streets of Paris with Pierre Bourdieu, and we are going to have a tête-à-tête lunch." A number of people recognize him and greet him. We enter a bistro, where he is quickly welcomed and given a table. He tells me that this bistro is far superior to others in the neighborhood.

From the moment we enter the bistro I realize that, unfortunately for me, the main dining space is exceptionally noisy. I have been suffering from an increasingly acute hearing loss since my mid-twenties. By the time I came to Paris my hearing aids were becoming useless in noisy spaces, and it will still be some time before I am literally saved by the wonderful cochlear implants. Having only conversed with Bourdieu in his quiet office space before, I haven't had the chance to share with him how deaf I am in noisier environments. While we are waiting for the plat du jour that he has recommended, Bourdieu starts talking about the difficulties associated with interviewing, and particularly the difficulties of knowing where and how to position tape recorders on the table and the many problems his team has had with malfunctioning tape recorders. He and his colleagues are working on what will become *La misère du monde*. I am putting all my energy into hearing what he is saying, so I am just staring at him and not saying much beyond nodding. He notices that he is monologizing; he stops and asks, "Mais . . . peut-être que je vous ennuie?" (But . . . maybe I am boring you?). After a moment of being embarrassed by his question, I explain to him that I am severely deaf and struggling to hear. Bourdieu inquires more about my deafness, but now he is articulating himself clearly and slowly. He does so very matter-of-factly, and I appreciate how quickly he has adapted his speech to my disability. I am also very grateful that I can hear him better, and that we are finally having a two-way conversation. Still, for a long while, all I can think about is the absurdity of the moment: Here I am, living the ultimate intellectual fantasy of my undergraduate years, sitting in Paris, in a bistro, with a famous French intellectual that I admire, and he's asking me if he is boring me.

Ever since, whenever I am reading or writing about Pierre Bourdieu, I cannot do so without imagining him leaning forward and asking me, "But . . . maybe I am boring you?" And I want to say to him what I felt I should have said back then: "You've got to be kidding me!" So, in many ways, this is my "you've got to be kidding me" book. It recounts the anything-but-boring experience I have had thinking about Bourdieu's work and thinking with it as I have deployed it in my research.

This rich experience did not begin when I started reading Bourdieu in the late 1970s and mid-1980s. At that time, in the academic milieus I interacted with as a student in Australia, Bourdieu was read either as a sociologist of the relation between class and education or as a general theorist of practice who tried to move away from structuralism. As to myself, I mainly read him through, and compared him to, Karl Marx as a sociologist of class domination. I was unaware of Bourdieu's refusal to be read as a theorist, and his insistence on the importance of empirical research as the necessary ground for thinking about his work. Nor was I cognizant of the importance of coming to terms with the philosophical questionings that were behind much of his conceptualizations. I became far more attentive to their significance once I sat in on some of his lectures. This dual insistence on the importance of both the empirical and the philosophical can superficially appear to be contradictory. Yet, reading Bourdieu by taking this twofold emphasis seriously, one begins to realize that rather than leaving one stranded or torn between two irreconcilable directions, the entanglement of the empirical and the philosophical is in fact one of the core productive/generative principles present in his work. Learning how it worked unlocked more fully for me the complexity and potency of Bourdieu's concepts. Increasingly these concepts began to unravel a rich terrain of analytical problematics that helped to open up my own empirical research, multiplying and complexifying the issues that emerged within it.

This book exposes some of these issues and the analytical concepts associated with them. I try to show how the concepts worked to provide new perspectives on, and insights into, my own empirical material. It is an invitation into some of the philosophico-theoretical dimensions of Bourdieu's ideas, but it is philosophy/theory as activated and thought out in the midst of research processes. As such, while the book is theoretical in its main subject matter, it is less so in its form and style. In many parts I try to tell the kind of stories that say "Look at the interesting things that Bourdieu made me think while I was researching"—that is, describing the process of thinking with Bourdieu as my research was unfolding rather than focusing on the end product of such a process.

It is perhaps important to say explicitly and right from the start that I am not into idealizing thinkers. I hope this will become clear throughout the text. From my very first publication on Bourdieu, I highlighted the fact that I am not inclined to treat thinkers and their thoughts as something one "adheres to," such as to become Bourdieusian, Foucauldian, or Latourian. Bourdieu's thinking, when useful, has never been sufficient to me. I have always found other thinkers as—and sometimes more—useful. Sometimes I have synthesized Bourdieu's thought with the thought of others, and sometimes I have done my own original theorizing (unbelievable, but true). That Bourdieu himself encouraged me along such a path was certainly important to me. When I gave him a draft of that early article to read, he highlighted the bit where I say, "Bourdieu is not a football team that one relates to as a 'supporter,'" and added the exclamation "Oui!" next to it. My students can vouch that if there is one thing I repeat religiously it is that one's primary allegiance should be to one's empirical data and not to a particular thinker. And while I am happy to glorify those dimensions of Bourdieu's work that are helping me think about my data, I am also more than happy to think differently and move elsewhere with my thinking if other thinkers or my own thinking can help me yield more from my data. That is why I have always related in a slightly puzzled way to people who dwell on what certain thinkers lack, such as the ubiquitous "Bourdieu doesn't have a theory of social change." Apparently it is raining social change and Bourdieu fails to account for it. Let me preempt those who have something similar to say when reading this book. My reply has always been "I've shown you how Bourdieu is useful to me thinking about x or y; if you are not interested in x or y, and if you don't find that he is useful to you thinking about whatever you are calling social change, the answer is very easy: don't think about your data with Bourdieu. Find someone who does help you, or, better still, produce your own theory."

Perhaps the above has a bearing on another question that has been on my mind while writing this book. What does it mean for someone like me to write "yet another book about a white male thinker" amid the rise of an academic culture of post-, anti-, and decolonialism that I consider both legitimate and necessary? Perhaps the fact that I see no contradiction between the two says something about me. But, as I will show in this book, I hope it says something about Bourdieu's work as well.[1]

Acknowledgments

In April 2022, I was presenting a seminar on Pierre Bourdieu's work at the Max Planck Institute for Social Anthropology in Halle, Germany. Something that was both funny and embarrassing happened.

I have been trying to finish a book on Bourdieu for so long now that I ritualistically mock myself about it. At Halle, I started my talk by jokingly telling my audience, "I am not going to tell you this is the very last version of the book I am writing about Pierre Bourdieu. I have been telling this to my students at the University of Melbourne for the last fifteen years, and every year I find myself writing yet another 'very last version of my book on Bourdieu.'" When I finished saying this, however, someone in the audience raised their hand and said, "My name is Samuel Williams, I am a senior researcher here, I was your student at the University of Sydney more than twenty years ago, and you were saying the same thing then as well." So . . . I'd better come clean about how long I've been fantasizing about this book. In fact, it would be hard for me to hide it. In my very first publication on Bourdieu ("Pierre Bourdieu in the Nineties"), which appeared in 1994, I talk about my failed fantasy of writing "the first English-language book on Bourdieu." In the flow of books on Bourdieu that followed and that is still flowing, the fantasy—or, rather, the successive fantasies—that ensued became of writing something about Bourdieu that hasn't already been said. This book inevitably carries the traces of this long history of fantasies.

Some elements of the text you have here began to take shape in the very first seminars I offered on the work of Bourdieu at the University of Sydney (1994–2007). I have also given various versions of this seminar as a visiting professor at the American University of Beirut, Harvard University, and the University of Copenhagen. Nonetheless, as already noted, this last rendition is largely the product of a series of seminars I gave at the University of Melbourne (2011, 2014, and 2017–22). As fate would have it, and following the presentation referred to above at the Max Planck Institute of Social Anthropology, I was given the opportunity to spend a year at the institute as a visiting fellow. I am thankful to Biao Xiang for encouraging me to give "one last series of seminars about my very last version of my book on Bourdieu" to help me wrap up the book. It worked.

I am indebted to the many students and colleagues who have attended the aforementioned seminars and who have discussed Bourdieu with me over the years. Geoffrey Mead, whose thesis on Bourdieu's habitus I supervised and who is now way more the real expert on Bourdieu around the block, has helped me fill holes and find appropriate quotes from Bourdieu's texts over many years. He has also helped me wrap up the whole final text. I am greatly indebted to him. A special mention ought to be made of my debt to my friend and colleague Michael Jackson, who invited me to teach courses on Bourdieu with him at both Harvard and the University of Copenhagen.

As always, I am thankful to have had my family around me throughout these many years of writing. My daughters have grown up with this work and even had Bourdieu negotiate a place in kindergarten for them when they lived with me in Paris. I am particularly grateful to my partner Caroline for reading and engaging with my work, and for enduring my detestable company when my writing is not going so well, especially during the despicable COVID-19 years.

Introduction: The Political Economy of Being...
and How to Analyze It

~~~~~~

Pierre Bourdieu often defended himself against a utilitarian understanding of his conception of practice. He particularly objected to those who took his claim that social agents "accumulate capital" to imply a conception of the individual akin to that of marginalist economics: someone always aiming to maximize profit.[1] He once retorted, "It is not true to say that everything that people do or say is aimed at maximizing their social profit; but one may say that they do it to perpetuate or to augment their social being."[2] This book grew out of an early conviction, reinforced over time, that a focus on this question of "perpetuation and augmentation of being," not so much as a conscious finality but as a dimension of all practices, allows readers a means of appreciating one of the richer frameworks of social analysis, which Bourdieu's theory of practice offers. It is a framework that highlights best the continuous interaction between metatheoretical/philosophical issues and empirical social research that is at the heart of his work. What this interaction entails is important to understand, even if it takes us—a bit too soon, perhaps—into difficult theoretical territory that requires more patience and attention to nuance than is often expected in a book's introduction. I find an early dive into such territory necessary to clarify to the reader the significance of the book's scope and structure.

The idea of an augmentation of being, and even the word *augmentation* itself, can be traced to Spinoza's definition of joy as an "augmentation" of the body's capacity to act.[3] As Spinoza put it,

> Joy is a man's passage from a lesser to a greater perfection.
> Sorrow is a man's passage from a greater to a less perfection.
> Exp[lanation]. I say a passage. For Joy is not perfection itself. If
>   a man were born with the perfection to which he passes, he
>   would possess it without an affect of Joy.
> This is clearer from the affect of Sadness, which is the opposite
>   of joy.[4]

Spinoza's affects are not about *how much you have* or *how well you are* but about *how much and how well you're being transformed*. It is the experience of change, the augmentation, the rate of accumulation, or, conversely, the decline in your efficiency that matters. Nonetheless, by placing this Spinozan notion of augmentation or diminution of being within a whole economy that involves not only the increase and decrease of being but also its production and distribution, we get a typically Bourdieusian mode of investing in philosophy and subverting it at the same time.

Many philosophers, particularly in the phenomenological tradition, like to talk about "being" with awe, and mostly in very absolutist terms. This makes questions such as "How much being does this person have?" or "What kind of being is society producing and distributing?" (a logical corollary of a conception of being as an economy) sound philosophically cheap and quasi-sacrilegious. Yet in coupling the word *augment* with the word *being* there lies a highly significant claim. It can be thought of as a kind of non-Shakespearian claim, since, from this perspective, "to be or not to be" is not the question. Here, being—or, social being to be precise—is not understood in "either/or" but in "more or less" terms. Satisfying and fulfilling forms of lives, in all their varieties, are not equally made available and distributed in and by society. Nor are the degrees to which they are satisfying and fulfilling. What's more, people do not just passively receive a certain *amount of being* from society. Though some might inherit a location and various material and symbolic resources that make the augmentation of their social being relatively easy, others must feverishly scrape the bottom of the barrel for a little bit of being. This is why, rather than "to be or not to be," the question becomes of the order of "How much can one be?"

An Existential Political Economy

This vision of society as an assemblage concerned with the production and distribution of social being, and the complementing image of social agents struggling to define, legitimize, and maximize whatever their conception of a viable life entails, permeates all of Bourdieu's work. This is what I am referring to as the political economy of being. It is an economy in that it is a process of production and distribution of ways of living articulated to a simultaneous process of assigning differential value to these ways of living. It is a *political* economy of being in that all those processes of production, distribution, and valorization are structured by relations of power and domination while being, at the same time, the subject and the outcome of political conflicts and struggles. Hubert Dreyfus and Paul Rabinow defined this as an "empirical existential analytics."[5] While this is made more explicit in Bourdieu's later works, like *Pascalian Meditations*,[6] it is already strongly present in the early texts. Even in the earliest writings on Algeria, one finds in Bourdieu's analysis of the encounter between French colonialism and the Algerian peasant an existential concern with the peasant's diminished being rather than the preoccupation, common at the time in the literature on imperialism, with economic deprivation and political subjugation. As the editors of the new edition of *Travail et travailleurs en Algérie* point out, the experiences analyzed in the book highlight the way the marginalized "find themselves dispossessed of the referents that gave meaning and direction to their lives."[7] In his inaugural lecture at the Collège de France, "A Lecture on the Lecture," Bourdieu follows the Durkheimian lineage to propose a vision of society as the purveyor of a meaningful life: "What is expected of God is only ever obtained from society, which alone has the power to justify you, to liberate you from facticity, contingency and absurdity."[8] In that lecture we not only glimpse an unequal distribution of being but identify being as something that the dominant class acquires at the *expense* of the dominated. The ability of the dominant class to increase its "access to being" is accompanied by the "descent of the dominated into nothingness or lesser being."[9]

The final chapter of *Pascalian Meditations* offers what is perhaps the most condensed exposition of this existential analytics. There Bourdieu tells us, "The social world gives what is rarest, recognition, consideration, in other words, quite simply, reasons for being." Accordingly, he points out, "one of the most unequal of all distributions, and probably, in any case, the most cruel, is the distribution of symbolic capital, that is, of social importance and of reasons for living," and "there is no worse dispossession, no worse privation, perhaps, than that of the losers in the symbolic struggle for recognition, for access to a socially recognized social being, in a word, to humanity."[10]

What Bourdieu means when he talks of "social being" varies.[11] As in the quote above, the augmentation of social being can mean an augmentation of recognition. But in many places, and as will be examined throughout this book, social being is also a question of self-realization and practical efficiency: the capacity to achieve what one sets out to do. Even though it is not a concept that Bourdieu has himself used, I have found the concept of *social viability* to be as useful to deploy as that of "social being," and a reasonable equivalent to it. Over the years, inspired by Bourdieu but encompassing the work of many others, I have tried to develop what I have called an anthropology of viability: an anthropology concerned with the way individuals and groups struggle to make their lives viable, whereby a viable life means an experience of life as worthwhile, fulfilling, and meaningful, as well as practically and symbolically satisfying.[12] Thus, without wishing to reduce Bourdieu to an anthropologist of viability, the present book can be usefully, or perhaps even best, read as my attempt to highlight what I see as Bourdieu's contribution to an anthropology of viability.

I will try to show how a struggle for viability is an enduring dimension of Bourdieu's analytical disposition toward society and one of the cornerstones of the analytical habitus he has bequeathed us. Analysts who inherit and internalize the modes of classification and the analytical practices this habitus entails start seeing struggles for being and viability in everything. Whether they are analyzing someone picking flowers in the countryside, talking about the latest Netflix series they have seen, looking for a job, or demonstrating for or against asylum seekers, they find themselves asking, What conception of a viable life is behind what is being done here? In what way is this practice an attempt to perpetuate or augment the social being of the person engaging in it? How do societies work to valorize certain conceptions of the viable life over others? How do they work to legitimize some and delegitimize others? How do they make available or restrict access to what certain conceptions of the viable life entails?

At the same time as it leads social analysts to see struggles for social viability everywhere, a Bourdieusian habitus is particularly conducive to making them see a distributional—that is, a "more or less" rather than an "either/or"—logic in everything. There is a long history of academics arguing against binary oppositions and either/or logic, but none are able to instill the opposite analytical vision of more or less as systematically as Bourdieu's analytical apparatus does. When social analysts internalize Bourdieu, the moment they hear someone making an either/or claim, they find themselves, almost unconsciously, critically deploying a more or less analytics.[13] In my work *White Nation*,[14] I deployed this logic to criticize the analytically taken-for-granted either/or logic of nationalism: "Are you or are you not Australian?" I showed that the claim itself is part of a logic of accumulation where what is at stake is a politics involving who is more and who is less, rather than who is and who is not Australian. Even when faced with what might appear as a banal identity claim such as "I am a man," a Bourdieusian analytical disposition invites one to approach it by asking, To what extent is such an identification an investment in and a pursuit of manhood? If it is, then in what way is this investment and pursuit a particular mode of augmenting one's social being and viability? What kind of social agent—that is, with what kind of social history and social trajectory—makes claims of being "more of a man" than others? What components are posited as necessary to accumulate to be "a man"? How are they accumulated? How is their possession unequally distributed in social space?

In this book I will elucidate some of the key questions raised by such an analytic vision. I will highlight the way societies are the sites of *economies* of being—that is, as noted, processes of production, distribution, valorization, accumulation, and loss of, as well as investment in, social being. But I will also highlight the way these economies are *political* economies—that is, both structured by power relations and the object of continuous struggles. Most important, perhaps, I will examine the way Bourdieu makes a conception of the social world as vague as "a political economy of social being" operational in empirical research. Last but not least, I will explore what it means to be a social scientist who is both a part of and professionally trying to make sense of the social world in this specific way.

The first thing to note when thinking about an economy of being is that it is not merely a matter of substituting *being* for terms commonly associated with the concept of economy as we know it (e.g., *money*, *wealth*, or *capital*). Thinking about an economy of being involves rethinking the very notion of economy. This is implied in Benedict de Spinoza's concept of "augmentation," which is not equivalent to the notion of "accumulation." For Spinoza, as for Bourdieu, certain forms of accumulation can lead to diminished rather than augmented being.[15] This is so even in the mundane way in which people say "Money doesn't bring happiness." In an economy of being it matters what you are accumulating. We know all too well today that a productivist economy that aims to accumulate development at any cost can lead to diminished being in the form of ecological misery. In an economy of being, how you are accumulating also matters: people who accumulate too slowly, or too quickly or voraciously, might witness a decline in their being.[16] This is similar to the way eating too much or too quickly can give one stomach pains. Thus, in an economy of being, the dominants do not aim just to get rich; they aim to flourish. And the dominated suffer from living diminished lives, which may or may not coincide with being poor. It is in that sense that Bourdieu and colleagues' *Weight of the World* offers the experience of men and women whose "social suffering" is grounded not in their poverty but in "the difficulties they have existing."[17]

If, from this perspective, Bourdieu's larger sociology aims to uncover the way societies constitute a space of struggle over how to define, produce, and distribute social viability, his conceptualization of practice is also formulated with a similar analytical horizon in mind: What makes a practice more or less conducive to the viability of those engaging in it? This is what this book focuses on. It explores how the key concepts that make up Bourdieu's theory of practice are all analytical components of this critical political economy of being.

Bourdieu and Philosophy

As noted earlier in this introduction, by emphasizing the overarching theme of a "critical political economy of being" I am also concerned with giving prominence to Bourdieu's dialogue with philosophical and metatheoretical issues and the way this dialogue is articulated to empirical research. As such, in each chapter, I endeavor to show the specific perspective on being and the struggle for viability that each of Bourdieu's concepts—be it habitus, *illusio*, capital, or field—offers. I explore the intellectual traditions with which each concept is in dialogue and, finally, the ways in which the concept, understood in this way, opens a new analytical horizon and allows for new research perspectives.

It is well known today that Bourdieu, like many other prominent French sociologists/anthropologists before him (Émile Durkheim, Claude Lévi-Strauss, and Lucien Lévy-Bruhl), was initially trained as a philosopher.[18] He was writing his thesis on Edmund Husserl under the supervision of Georges Canguilhem when he was conscripted into the French Army and deployed in Algeria.[19] There he morphed into an anthropologist and, later, a sociologist. It is not surprising therefore that there are many explicit and implicit critical dialogues with philosophy in Bourdieu's work. As he sees it, even though philosophy raises some of the more difficult questions about the world, social science, because it involves empirical investigations, offers a better space for thinking through such questions. But it can only do so when the social scientist is aware of the metatheoretical and philosophical issues they are confronting. As such, Bourdieu calls for, and sees himself as always engaging in, "fieldwork in philosophy."[20]

Despite the continuous presence of this philosophical dimension, the relation between Bourdieu's work and philosophy was hardly acknowledged in the early reception of his work, especially in the Anglophone academic world. It can be said that the relation became harder to avoid in later years because Bourdieu's work itself increasingly highlighted it.[21] It was becoming already more pronounced in *Practical Reason* and even more so in *Pascalian Meditations*. As such, this relation is the subject of a number of articles and books, and a whole conference was devoted to it.[22] Some philosophers have even claimed Bourdieu as one of their own, arguing that despite his stating that he is using philosophy to further a better sociology, there is enough evidence to ask whether, in fact, he has not found in sociology the best way to approach philosophy.[23] In a way, saying that Bourdieu is aiming for a sociologically grounded philosophy is just as true as saying that he is aiming for a more philosophically inspired sociology. At any rate, it makes the particular mode of interaction between philosophy and sociology that his work entails necessary to engage with right from the start. It is important for approaching Bourdieu in general, but particularly so to understand what it means for him to see social life as a struggle for what I have called the perpetuation and augmentation of being.

At one level, it can be said that Bourdieu sees in philosophy a type of aristocratic ethos, a mode of free thinking, unhampered by the mundane reality of the pleb and, as such, providing the philosopher with unlimited *jouissance*.[24] One can feel, reading Bourdieu, that he is not immune to the charm of this kind of ethos but that, at the same time, he is trying to resist it at any cost.[25] He does so via sociology, which is positioned as a kind of submission to a reality principle (empirical reality) that needs to be investigated as a price one has to pay to engage in decent thinking.[26]

This idea of philosophy as the unlimited *jouissance* of a thought that knows no empirical restraints is perhaps behind Jacques Derrida's reported quip that Bourdieu relates to philosophy as a man relates to his mistress. This is a pertinent characterization insofar as the traditional male imaginary of the mistress denotes not only a clandestine relation with someone but also a relation that provides one with more enjoyment than responsibility and a type of escape from the exigencies of social reality that are represented by married life. Nonetheless, one can say that after Bourdieu's critical severity toward Martin Heidegger in *The Political Ontology of Martin Heidegger*, toward Jean-Paul Sartre in *Outline of a Theory of Practice*, and toward Immanuel Kant in *Distinction*,[27] *Pascalian Meditations* represents a succumbing to the philosophical pleasure principle, where the relation to the mistress is brought out in the open.

As helpful as this opposition between reality and pleasure principles might be, there is another, more important dimension to Bourdieu's critical engagement with philosophical thought. It presents itself in his critique of what he has termed, after J. L. Austin, "scholastic reason." Detailing the meaning and the significance of this critique of scholasticism is important to fully understand the nature of Bourdieu's analytical categories and how they relate to the political economy of being that they aim to unpack. This is where the "patience and attention to nuance" that I have implored from the reader early in this introduction is at its most necessary.

The Problematic of Scholastic Reason

In *Sense and Sensibilia*, Austin refers to what he calls the "scholastic view." He illustrates it with the example of the "erudite," who, when looking for the meaning of a word, produces an inventory of all possible meanings outside any particular context of usage.[28] Bourdieu develops his critique of scholastic reason through a thorough reflection on the conditions of possibility and implications of this capacity to look at things outside any particular context of usage, which is encouraged at school and later professionalized in universities. In opposition to scholastic reason is precisely the thought that is produced within a particular context of usage, what Bourdieu calls "practical reason." The latter, he argues, is the reason that dominates everyday social life and that people produce while engaging in tasks, big and small, directed toward practical ends—from walking to the station, to cooking for one's family, to operating on a patient, to planning a demonstration.

The opposition between the scholastic and the practical is far from absolute, and it is easy to find cases that do not fit. It goes without saying, for instance, that engaging in thinking as part of a university job can readily be seen as a particular type of everyday practice rather than something opposed to everyday practices as such. And it is not the case that practical reason is free from scholastic ruminations. Like all binary oppositions, it works best to help us think of a certain difference rather than create an empirically strict, and strictly binary, classificatory system.

In much the same way, it is useful to think of the opposition between abstract/metatheoretical and concrete/applied thought as a binary that coincides with the scholastic and practical binary. But it would be wrong to take this to mean that those thinking from within the university do not think practically or that those engaging in everyday practices do not think metatheoretically. An example of practical reason is the knowledge that an electrician is producing and deploying to install or fix your home's electrical circuits. This knowledge can be usefully opposed to an abstract meditation on various conceptions of the nature of electricity and its relation to the vital forces of life, which is more of the order of scholastic reason. Nonetheless, though the electrician might well engage in abstract metatheoretical thinking while contemplating a problem encountered as they fix your circuit, their abstract reasoning, insofar as they are engaging in it in relation to fixing your circuit, is subordinate to that practical function.

Thus, the best differentiating criterion that can help us understand what Bourdieu is aiming to achieve remains the difference in the finalities and ends of different practices, which are also the finalities and ends of the thinking articulated toward these practices. Scholastic reason involves a mode of thinking about the world for the sake of thinking about the world. Practical reason is more of the order of instrumental reason; it characterizes the thought that is deployed as part of deeds that are more functional, pragmatic, and—at the risk of sounding tautological—practical.

To be immediately clear, for Bourdieu, the problem is not that scholastic knowledge is *bad* and practical knowledge *good*. Far from it. The word *scholastic* itself derives from the notion of *skholè*, advanced by Plato to describe a position that puts the thinker at a distance from the urgencies and necessities of social life.[29] In this sense, scholastic reason today is the product of a type of thinking that thrives in those areas of the university where people still engage in what is referred to as pure science (which includes pure social science). These areas can still be thought of with an "ivory tower" imaginary and its intimations of detachment from urgent practical problem-solving. Even if such a university life is no more than a cliché in most universities today, Bourdieu believed that the kind of thinking that university life implies continues to leave its imprint on academic thought, precisely because of the structural position of pure scientific research vis-à-vis society. Academics engaging in pure science remain those thinkers who can take a distance from the social processes around them. They are not doing any time-restricted applied research for a government, a company, or any other organization. Relative to other researchers they are still given *the time to take their time* in order to think. Bourdieu, like Plato, sees this as something positive. The best social science is a social science that is free from urgent social problem-solving imperatives imposed on it by nonacademic economic, political, or even social forces. Bourdieu's anti-neoliberal activism in later years was motivated by the desire to protect this freedom "from urgent social problem-solving" and its conditions of possibility from what he saw as governmental attempts at undermining it by imposing national-interest imperatives.[30] Thus, Bourdieu is clear that his critique of scholastic reason should not be seen as an ethical or political condemnation of the scholastic position as such.[31] It is, after all, a position that marks all academic thought, including his own. Rather, the object of his critique is a common tendency in scholastic thought to be blind to its specificity.[32] This ends up producing a series of scholastic biases and fallacies that limit the very gains that such a position can afford the thinker.

For Bourdieu, this blindness to the specificity of one's reasoning about the world is first and foremost a blindness to the specificity of one's *perspective* on the world. Here the prime examples are those philosophers who philosophize about being and life in "oracle mode" (and as if no one in particular is living the life they are referring to). The biggest problem with scholastic thought is that it often fantasizes itself to be perspectiveless. It becomes clear at this point that while Bourdieu often criticizes philosophy in general, his particular targets are the same perspectiveless philosophers famously admonished by Friedrich Nietzsche when he wrote,

> Henceforth, my dear philosophers, let us be on guard against the dangerous old conceptual fiction that posited a "pure, will-less, painless, timeless knowing subject"; let us guard against the snares of such contradictory concepts as "pure reason," "absolute spirituality," "knowledge in itself": these always demand that we should think of an eye that is completely unthinkable, an eye turned in no particular direction, in which the active and interpreting forces, through which alone seeing becomes seeing something, are supposed to be lacking; these always demand of the eye an absurdity and a nonsense. There is only a perspective seeing, only a perspective "knowing."[33]

While Bourdieu's perspectivism was born in interaction with many philosophers other than Nietzsche, and particularly philosophers of science like Gaston Bachelard and Georges Canguilhem, it is hard to overstate how important Nietzsche's perspectivism is to him. In one of his earliest Collège de France lectures Bourdieu explicitly declares that "insofar as the social world is concerned, perspectivism as conceived by Nietzsche is unsurpassable."[34] One needs to take this statement seriously, and it can be said that without a good understanding of the way this perspectivism affects his outlook, one cannot capture the scope of Bourdieu's analytical categories and would only be scratching their surface. By the same token, it is this perspectivism that helps us explain best how Bourdieu conceives of the interaction between philosophy and the social sciences and how this very interaction shapes his own analysis of the "perpetuation and augmentation of being." Three dimensions of Nietzsche's perspectivism are of most importance to him: first, the need to acknowledge perspective; second, the importance of perspectival multiplicity; and third, an ontological conception of perspectivism.

Taking Perspectivism Seriously

To take perspectivism seriously means first and foremost to take seriously Nietzsche's emphasis on the *only* in the claim "there is *only* a perspective seeing, *only* a perspective 'knowing.'" Perspectivism is one of those things that everyone agrees with but very few rigorously put in practice. Let me insert a brief example here. I get many prospective research students from a variety of disciplines who come to me and say that they want to work "on multiculturalism" or "on racism." When I ask "From whose perspective?" it turns out that this was not something that was considered. For instance, one can work on racism from the perspective of racists and one can work on racism from the perspective of the racialized. One can, of course, work on racism tout court, but this itself assumes either a governmental perspective or indeed a scholastic perspective whereby one is hovering over the phenomenon, able to gaze at racism as a process or a structure. Despite sometimes lapsing into an oppositional mode of thinking,[35] Bourdieu, on the whole, does not necessarily invite us to prefer one perspective over another. What is more consistent with his approach is to see him as stressing the need to be clear—to clarify to oneself and to one's readers what perspective is being researched.

As there is always, in Bourdieu's writing, more than a hint of a competitive attempt to dethrone philosophy from its position as the aristocrat of the human sciences, this perspectivism becomes particularly important: it brings sociology right into the heart of philosophy. This is so because perspectivism means that there is nothing more "meta" than sociology itself. Once we say that all thoughts about the world are generated from a particular perspective on the world, we are saying that any thinking about the world, including philosophical thinking, necessitates a sociology: an analysis of where *in* the world—that is, from which *social* location—a perspective on the world emanates from and how this social location leaves its imprint on what is thought. The problem with philosophy—or, rather, with the dominant mode of doing philosophy—is that it fails on all these counts. Even if one accepts that the aim of philosophy is to reach a certain knowledge that transcends particular perspectives, and Bourdieu does accept that, there is no escape from the fact that this transcendence is only possible from a particular social location and the perspective that it allows. When it refuses to see itself in such a perspectivist way, philosophy is unable to understand what constitutes its specificity, with all the gains it affords us as well as their limits. By the same token, it fails to understand its difference from the practical nonscholastic reason that is far more prevalent in the world. Consequently, Bourdieu's critique goes on to maintain that an analytical thought—or a "diagnostic" thought, as Michel Foucault called it—that lacks such a sociological perspective on itself ends up positing that everyone is engaging in the kind of invariable, universal reasoning that is peculiar to it. Or as Bourdieu formulaically puts it, it ends up "projecting its own particular relation to the object into the object."[36] That is, it imagines itself talking about the whole world while, in fact, it is only talking about its own world.

Thus, Bourdieu argues, social thinkers have to ask themselves whose perspective on the world they are taking to be the object of their research. There are many perspectives on the world to choose from, whether it is the perspectives of individuals or collectives, whether these are contingent or structural, and so on. But as a first step, social researchers need to ask themselves if they want to take their own perspective on life as their object of reflection, or if they want to analyze those nonacademic perspectives on life where practical reason prevails. For Bourdieu, the answer is clear: If social thinkers are to write about people's struggle for "being" in the world, and they want their thought to be relevant to those struggles, they do not want to write about a kind of being that consists of sitting in an office and contemplating the hard questions of life. They want to research those regions of life where practical reason prevails.[37]

The differentiation between scholastic and practical perspectives is akin to taking a particular sport and differentiating between the perspective of the people engaging in the sport, the players, and the perspective of the professional commentators observing it from the spectators' stand. For Bourdieu, insofar as this analogy is relevant, what is true of a sports game is also true of the "game of life": unlike those playing the game, philosophers and social scientists all occupy spectator seats, and anything they say and write about the game they are observing is marked by their perspective as spectators. As he puts it in *The Logic of Practice*, "The inadequacy of scholarly discourse derives from its ignorance of all that its theory of the object owes to its theoretical relation to the object, as Nietzsche . . . suggested: 'Kant, like all philosophers, instead of envisaging the aesthetic problem from the point of view of the artist (the creator), considered art and the beautiful purely from that of the "spectator," and unconsciously introduced the "spectator" into the concept "beautiful.""[38]

The first kind of fallacy that Bourdieu wants to avoid, and that he accuses the worst kind of philosophical scholastic thinking of engaging in, is to comment on how one is experiencing life as a spectator and assume that one is commenting about life in general. It's like writing a book titled *How to Live a Better Life* about how to be more comfortable in your spectator seat, and how to access the kiosk to buy yourself beer and some chips as efficiently as possible, without being conscious of the specificity of the life you are writing about, and assuming that your writing is about everyone's lives and should be of value to everyone, including the players. For Bourdieu, there is nothing wrong with writing about what one's life as a spectator is like, as long as one is aware of the specificity of what one is writing about. But if one wants to claim that one's writing is relevant to those who are engaging in the game, one has to take the life of those playing the game as one's object.

Yet scholastic problems are not eliminated simply by being clear about whose life experience is being analyzed. Even when one takes life from the perspective of the players as one's object, another form of scholastic fallacy appears: to observe the game and comment on the players, but to see them only from one's perspective as an observer, without having a sense of what it feels like for them as players. We, spectators of sport, often engage in minor forms of this scholastic fallacy when, let us say, a player approaches the goal in a football match, shoots from a short distance and yet misses, and we exclaim, "How could you?" What seemed so simple from a spectator position could have been much harder to execute "in the heat of the game," where exhaustion, nerves, limits of bodily reflexes, a different field of vision, and many other things are at play that we spectators are not experiencing. The opposite can also be true. What seems very hard to achieve from the perspective of the spectator might have been very easy to execute from the perspective of a player with years of training. Bourdieu wants a social science that is more phenomenological in this regard, one that is more able to apprehend life as lived by and as unfolding before the players playing it. The difficulty for those who want to think with him is that he also wants that social science to be distant from the players, analytical and structural. But this is only difficult if one has internalized an opposition between phenomenology and structuralism. For, at another level, one can say that all Bourdieu is offering is a version of participant observation. But it is a philosophically enmeshed version of participant observation with a particularly acute awareness of the perspectivist gymnastics and rigor that are required for engaging in such an inherently multiperspectival mode of researching and analyzing.

14 　　To be clear, then: Despite the issues his demand generates, Bourdieu not only sees the position of the observer and spectator of the game as inevitable—this is where social analysts are structurally located—but also sees it as necessary and useful. It is the source of perceptions and understandings that the players involved in the game do not have access to. The spectators/analysts have a macroperspective that, depending on their sophistication, professionalism, and training as analysts, allows for important insights into certain realities affecting the game that only they have the time and the skills to examine and perceive clearly. The issue for Bourdieu is that unless one has at the same time a phenomenological understanding of reality from the perspective of the players, like that described above, one cannot understand how these macrorealities are experienced by the players. Without such a perspective, the analyst is still bound to produce knowledge that is of interest only to other analysts and of little or no interest to the players of the game. As such, one can say that Bourdieu is interested in analytically relevant knowledge. He wants to analyze the way players are engaged in a political economy of being, but he wants an analysis that players can find relevant and of use in their struggles to augment their social viability. In wanting to combine a macro- and microanalytics of practice, in wanting to understand the game from a detached perspective as well as how it is experienced by the players, and in wanting his categories to be both analytical and of practical relevance, it can be said that Bourdieu wants social scientists to produce knowledge akin to that deployed by coaches who also work from this double perspective. To be sure, *akin to* does not mean "the same" but rather "of the same order." It is a knowledge that wants to push players to see more than they can see if they are left to their own devices and, as such, it is a knowledge that uses categories that are outside people's everyday perspectives but that is nonetheless aimed at widening that perspective by never losing touch with what the perspective entails. This is another dimension that makes for the

specificity of Bourdieu's notion of "participant observation." He not only wants the *method* of obtaining data to be a variety of participant observation but also wants the *result* of the analysis itself to be observational and participatory. That is, while many undertake participant observation to produce texts that are solely for other academics, Bourdieu wants the text and the analytical categories that he produces to be themselves invitations to *observe* that *participate* in enhancing the being of those who read them.

To maximize this possibility, Bourdieu wants social thinkers, whether philosophers or social scientists, to acknowledge that even when they have the best intentions of understanding the game from the perspective of those playing it, and even when they equip themselves to do so theoretically and with well-acquired data, they can never eliminate the effect of their structural position on the knowledge that they are producing. They therefore need to examine and labor at how they produce knowledge and how they communicate it. This is why Bourdieu argues the need to integrate yet another perspective to all the other perspectives above. It is what he refers to as "reflexivity."[39] Social analysts have to be analytical observers of themselves as they are observing others playing the game if they want their categories to be relevant and communicable despite these categories coming from outside people's everyday reality. They need to fully analyze and understand their relation to the object, which is that of the "outsider who has to procure a substitute for practical mastery in the form of an objectified model."[40]

This, in a way, is a version of Nietzsche's perspectivist pluralism. Social thinkers have to continuously split themselves in three so that one part of them is apprehending a practice from the perspective of the players, one part of them is apprehending the macrosocial grounds in which the play is happening, and one part of them is devising a perspective on the totality these parts comprise. In much the same way, each of Bourdieu's analytical categories has to be seen as the scene where the interplay between these perspectives is played out. When we read and analytically deploy habitus, *illusio*, capital, or field and fail to see the work that Bourdieu is trying to make them do—and to make us, the readers and users of these categories, do—we are reading them and deploying them in a truncated fashion. There is nothing necessarily wrong with this. From my own personal perspective, as I have already indicated, I don't have a desire to engage in or advocate a "religious" faithfulness to an author's intentions, but it is clearly better if one is aware of how partial one's interpretation is. For there is no doubt that for a fuller appreciation of the scope of Bourdieu's categories we need to appreciate that they are always inviting us to see things, at the same time, from the people's practical perspective, understood phenomenologically from the inside; the outsider analytical perspective of social scientists on the people's practical perspective; and the reflexive perspective on social scientists having a perspective on the people's perspective.

There is one final dimension of Nietzsche's perspectivism that finds its way into Bourdieu's work and has important consequences for how we perceive the interplay of perspectives described above. It is the former's ontological variety of perspectivism. For Nietzsche, a perspective is not an angle on an already existing meaningful reality. Social objects and social realities come into being through the process of relating and having a perspective on them. For Nietzsche, without an active seeing there is nothing much to see. It is only because we have a perspective that embodies *active and interpreting forces* that seeing becomes seeing *something*. From this Nietzschean standpoint, when a social scientist produces a category such as *social structure*, this structure comes into being as a reality through the analytical perspective that has a purpose in bringing it forth. Its reality is associated with its analytical pertinence. At the same time, this does not make it an analytical fiction any more than an *atomic structure* is. It points to something that exists and that has causal powers even for those who do not experience it or who experience it differently and have another language to account for it within their own reality.

As we shall later see, this theoretical realism has important ramifications for a Bourdieusian conception of politics. But it is also important to help us understand how Bourdieu's analytical categories function. As with the example of the social scientist above, it is clear that Bourdieu sees his categories as analytical categories. People do not walk around with a consciousness of their habitus or their *illusio*, but they do walk around with a consciousness of something that habitus and *illusio* allude to. The latter are nonetheless theories of the social subjects (or the "social agents," as Bourdieu prefers to call them) produced by a social scientist to account for the nature of their agency. But, yet again, they are not *just* theories, if by *theory* one means something constructed intellectually to account for reality. There is more to them than that. For if perspectives are ontologically productive and specific, the idea that Bourdieu's categories are, as I have argued above, a meeting ground for three perspectives will mean that the categories are the meeting ground of three realities. They embody the reality of the person or group engaging in a particular practice, the reality of that part of the social scientist observing that person or group, and the reality of that part of the social scientist observing herself observing the person or group. This can easily start to sound farcical if not thought out properly. Suffice to say at this introductory stage that Bourdieu doesn't just want to "reflect" on the reality of the people's struggle for being that he is analyzing. He wants the analytic world he brings forth to participate in this struggle. He wants his analytic labor to open up a reality that helps people augment their being. That is, he wants his categories to be participatory in the processes they are analyzing.

To summarize what has been highlighted in this introduction, we can say that Bourdieu's categories articulate three broad concerns. First, they aim to offer an analytics of the way a particular dimension of practice is conducive to the social viability of those engaging in it. Second, they aim to be autoreflexive categories: they are the seats of an interperspectival gymnastics, constantly elucidating the epistemological and ontological presuppositions and processes they are part of. Third, they are in continuous dialogue with the philosophical traditions that have reflected on the analytical ground they are concerned with: through them Bourdieu wants to demonstrate how empirically oriented research offers the ground for metatheoretical reflections. To fail to see how all this is at work when concepts like habitus, *illusio*, capital, field, and symbolic violence are deployed is to be merely scratching surfaces.

Chapter 1 stresses the importance of understanding *practice* as the very mode of existing in the world. But while practical being can take many forms, the chapter stresses the importance of routinized practices. The latter are the very stuff from which the social world is made. The chapter explores why and how, for Bourdieu, routinized, habitual practices are defined by degrees of efficiency that reflect degrees of complicity with the social world. It goes on to describe how habitus offers a theorization of humans insofar as they are social beings subjectively oriented toward the augmentation of their practical efficiency and complicity with reality. The chapter explores how the concept of habitus involves a dialogue with a vitalist tradition that sees the viability of life as capacity to act: energy, power, efficiency, and force.

Chapter 2 starts by highlighting that, for Bourdieu, the way societies continue to reproduce their basic structures despite the immense changes that they undergo over time is of the order of the magical. Part of the magic is the way routinized social practices are continually generating new strategies to meet new situations and yet manage to reproduce the social world in the very process of doing so. The chapter stresses how important it is to understand that habitus is a theory of what we are as social subjects such that we are continually performing this magical trick. As such, the chapter highlights the ontological nature of habitus as a real, generative structure that constitutes us and where practical dispositionality emerges as a social force. The chapter finishes with an autoanalysis of my own deafness as a way to understand the potentials and limits of habitus.

Chapter 3 explores the way, with the concept of *illusio*, that Bourdieu is broadly in dialogue with the phenomenological tradition that delineates something like an "existential viability." The concept offers us a window into the dimension of life where social viability is primarily associated with the existence of a raison d'être, something to live for. The chapter examines the notion of *investing the self* in a meaningful life. It explores three orders of meaningfulness encompassed by *illusio*: the order of intelligibility, where to speak of a meaningfulness of life and of social reality is to speak of them as making sense, as not being absurd; the order of purposefulness, where to speak of meaningful life is to highlight having a life with aims and a sense of direction; and, finally, the order of importance, where meaningfulness points to a life that one takes seriously.

Chapter 4 examines the angle that Bourdieu's concept of capital offers on his economy of being. The chapter begins by showing that there is a sense in which the accumulation of capital points to an accumulation of efficiency and an accumulation of meaningfulness and as such offers another take on habitus and *illusio*. It is only with the notion of symbolic capital that we have a new dimension of viability associated with recognition. Here Bourdieu is in dialogue with a largely Hegelian and post-Hegelian tradition that has always been concerned with such questions. The chapter explores the way the accumulation of capital points to a *phallic modality of being* in which recognition and legitimacy are associated with the possession of distinction.

Chapter 5 deals with Bourdieu's concept of field. If humans aim to augment their being by augmenting their practical efficiency—by securing a sense of purpose in life and by seeking recognition from others—they do so as beings born in an already existing social space demanding particular forms of practical efficiency, offering particular paths of self-realization, and offering recognition for certain forms of capital more than others. This social space is already marked by various modes of domination and by certain routinized forms of distribution that create enduring (structured) social divisions. This is what Bourdieu calls "fields."

Highlighting the social nature of being and viability means, first and foremost, that social being is irreducible to individuals. It is associated with certain structural locations. These locations offer in themselves certain forms of social being in the form of inheritance of resources but also in the form of inheritance of capacities to augment one's inheritances. Being associated with particular structural locations means that social viability, as opposed to individual viability, is a class matter. Furthermore, because people are born in particular locations within these fields, the way fields are structured and organized has a causal effect on people's capacity to augment their being. The field is not just a scene where things happen; it has its own dynamic and the forces that emanate from it, as magnetic fields are causal in themselves.

The book's conclusion deals with the way Bourdieu conceives the relation between viability and domination. The latter, it will be argued, is ultimately conceived as the ability to institute a social ecology in which one can augment one's being. The conclusion highlights an often-missed ontological dimension present in the work of Bourdieu. It can be said that, for him, we are ultimately autoecological beings: we generate our own ecology, that is, the environment in which we thrive. In the conclusion we examine the various forms that domination takes in this process of making and unmaking reality, and how each form of domination affects the production and distribution of being at both macro- and microlevels. The conclusion then highlights another important dimension of viability treated by Bourdieu: the dimension of "reflexivity." Reflexivity, in its most general sense, is the capacity to reflect on the unfolding of one's own being. It is about how well one understands one's location, one's inheritances, one's capacities, and one's social determinations and the particular way all of these bring our reality into existence. It is what Bourdieu has sometimes referred to in his lectures as "lucidity." The conclusion ends with a reflection on the relation between lucidity and viability.

Social Efficiency
and Social Complicity

~~~~~~

Given the interrelated nature of Pierre Bourdieu's key concepts, choosing any one of them as a point of entry into his political economy of being can be seen as purely arbitrary. Nonetheless, beginning with habitus, as many exposés of Bourdieu's work do, makes obvious sense. Perhaps this is because, along with cultural capital, it is the concept people associate most with Bourdieu, his "signature theoretical concept."[1] Or perhaps it is because habitus is most intimately linked to Bourdieu's theory of "practice," which is what gave his work its distinction in the era of structuralism when it emerged.[2] In any case, it makes sense from the perspective of this book to begin unpacking the political economy of being by elucidating how Bourdieu theorizes the practicing social agent that is at the center of this economy. For habitus is, before all else, a theory about what such practicing social agents *are*—that is, what properties they possess that allow them to engage in the kind of practices they engage in. *Theory*, *properties*, *practicing*, *social*, and *agent* are not random words. Each aims to convey something important about both habitus and the conception of human viability that underlies it and that it aims to capture sociologically.

Most explorations of Bourdieu's habitus rightly highlight the way it accounts for how the human body, by internalizing society through a historical process of sedimentation of habitual practices, becomes a quasi-unconscious practical decision-maker.[3] As Bourdieu puts it, "social agents are endowed with habitus," which he refers to as "schemes of perception, appreciation and action" that are "inscribed in their bodies by past experiences."[4] These systems enable people to go about their daily lives doing things in a habitual manner without spending much time thinking them through in a calculative manner. *Unconscious* here only tangentially alludes to something like Sigmund Freud's notion of the unconscious. One can also speak of "unrationalized" or "minimally rationalized" practices (which, to be clear, are neither arational nor irrational).

And Besides Structure and Agency, What Else?

Partly because of Bourdieu's emphasis on unconscious schemes, habitus is often introduced by foregrounding its negotiation of the structure/agency problematic. And there is no doubt that, when Bourdieu introduced the concept, this was (and continues to be) one of its central analytical functions: to move away from both a voluntaristic, ahistorical conception of volitional subjects and a structuralist understanding in which the presence of a social agent appears to make no difference on the structurally determined unfurling of social processes.[5] Bourdieu's preference to conceive people as social *agents* rather than social *subjects* is part of the same concern. He feels that *agent* conveys the idea of an individual "preceded by their social definition."[6] He argues that the notion of *subject* invites a facile conception of practice, present in both commonsense understanding of practices and in various "philosophies of consciousness." Such a notion sees the consciousness of the person initiating a practice, such that the reasons they have for doing it are the practice's starting point (i.e., its cause), failing to see the creativity as emanating from the deployment of the historically and socially formed mind-body assemblage in its totality.[7]

For Bourdieu, the idea of an always already practically enmeshed agent precludes any a priori locating of human agency in a mentally biased ahistorical capacity to make "choices," whether "rational" or "free." To take practicing agents as a starting point is to consider both rationality and freedom as themselves socially and historically constituted and situated in practice. They are deeply embedded in the very way social agents move and interact in space and time. Therefore, "freedom" and "rationality" cannot be taken as starting points of anything, as if they are floating around in a space-time-free location waiting to be activated and brought into the social when needed. Just as important, not everyone is endowed with the same capacity for freedom and rationality even when—or, rather, particularly because—these freedoms and rationalities are historically produced in and by the social. In short, there is an economy of the production and distribution of practical freedom and practical rationality that means that these, like just about everything else for Bourdieu, are not distributed equally among the members of a social formation.[8] They are part of the economy of being that needs to be unpacked and analyzed—not the starting point of analysis. By the same token, in highlighting "agency" Bourdieu also wanted to avoid the concept of "actor," which implies a "role" and therefore reduces agents to people merely enacting a part in a prewritten script.[9] He saw Louis Althusser's famed structuralist conception of the agent as a support (*Träger*) for the structure as an example of this reductionism.[10]

I am not sure whether a concept of *agent* convincingly avoids the problems of either the socially undetermined deliberating subject or the structurally overdetermined one. *Agent* can still imply an unhampered agency, and it could be argued that the notion of *subject* is better than *agent* in that it allows for the dialectic of "being subjected to / determined by something" and "being the subject/initiator of an act." In opposition to those who make facile claims about Bourdieu "merely" providing a version of determinism, Laurent Perreau makes a good case for Bourdieu having despite himself an actual theory of the subject.[11]

In this chapter, while I will stick to Bourdieu's preference and speak of "agents," I want to decenter, or at least try to decenter, the issue of structure and agency. I know from my teaching that it is not an easy thing to do. The issue has an addictive quality to it for those who are beginning to think socially: People just like to go on and on arguing about freedom versus determinism. While this is, needless to say, a serious issue, and its unresolved nature generates many interesting propositions, the bulk of what passes as commentary on it is not. It is like those endless "Is there a reality or is it all in our mind?" debates that laypeople like to have. As my flippant tone makes clear, I have to admit that the structure/agency debate does very little to tickle my own analytical imagination. I always experience it as stalled and sterile, and I have never been able to see Bourdieu's view on structure and agency as a "correction" of Jean-Paul Sartre's essentialized freedom, or of Claude Lévi-Strauss's structural world. I feel more inclined to see it as an approach that highlights a different and complementary rather than an incommensurate dimension of the social world from the ones emphasized by Sartre and Lévi-Strauss, respectively.[12] Personally, I was first introduced to the debate as an undergraduate by R. W. Connell when she taught me first-year sociology in the late 1970s. And I have not felt that we have advanced much beyond the issues she raised in teaching and later published in her famous "black box" article in the early 1980s.[13]

Regardless of my personal views, I think it can be recognized that the debate around the question of structure and agency has been going for long enough that the possibility of original reflection it offers seems to have been exhausted. The repetition of variations on the same arguments regarding the topic has become wearing. Bourdieu himself seems to have lost interest in centering this problematic in his later work. One senses in this work a certain resignation and a loss of hope of ever producing a way of speaking about structure/agency that does not hit a brick wall of déjà vu arguments. I believe this dissatisfaction was always there, even if not foregrounded.

The narrator and central character in Olga Tokarczuk's novel *Drive your Plow over the Bones of the Dead* is made to describe a writer thus: "In a way, people like her, those who wield a pen, can be dangerous. At once a suspicion of fakery springs to mind—that such a Person is not him or herself, but an eye that's constantly watching, and whatever it sees it changes into sentences; in the process it strips reality of its most essential quality— its inexpressibility."[14] In a certain way, Bourdieu feels the same about the various attempts at expressing with words the tensions, antinomies, and contradictions relating to the experiences of freedom and determination that are inherent to practice. While in conversation with Loïc Wacquant, describing the way habitus negotiates the question of structure and agency, Bourdieu finishes a response by saying that he is not satisfied with what he has just said because, "despite the qualifications I have attached to it, verbally and mentally . . . I am still inclined or drawn to simplifications which, I fear, are the inescapable counterpart of 'theoretical talk.'"[15] There is, then, for him, something about practice that always escapes the attempts to translate it into conceptual terms. It is where "speaking" and "theorizing" about practices highlight the ontological gap that separates scholastic and practical reason.[16] Thus, it is not that certain aspects of practice are badly formulated; it is more that there is something about them that cannot be re-presented within the symbolic order. One even gets a sense from Bourdieu that some of the conceptual difficulties of thinking about determinism versus freedom, structure versus agency, are not problems inherent to practices, as much as problems created by the failure and deficiencies of the language we have available to us to speak about practice.[17] These deficiencies cannot be remedied, for they are the product of the inevitable ontological gap between the conceptualization of practice and practice as it is lived. I am hoping that approaching habitus from the perspective of a political economy of being and highlighting it as a theorization of the agents' practical affinity with the social world will help us avoid dwelling too much on the dead ends of the structure/agency problematic and will help us raise different productive points of discussion concerning both society and social agents.

I began this chapter by noting that, for Bourdieu, habitus is a theory of the practicing social agent, and that all these terms are of equal importance to him. In fact, of these, none are as important to keep in mind right from the start as *practicing*. After all, it is the term with which Bourdieu's overall theory is associated. In this chapter, I will be concentrating on the nature of habitual social practices and the way social agents accumulate being via these social practices. To be clear, habitual practices are not habitus. Habitus is what generates habitual practices. I am hoping that this mode of beginning with the product rather than the producer, as it were, will make for a better understanding of habitus and its place within Bourdieu's political economy of being.

On Practical Being

For Bourdieu, to speak of "practicing" agents, or agents of/in practice, does not only mean an interest in people or groups insofar as they are doing something specific at a particular moment that one can call practice. It is also an invitation to see social agents in a continually practical relation to the world. Practice is not something that one sometimes does and sometimes does not do. It is the very mode of existing and being enmeshed in the world. Being is always practical being. We are always unfolding and deploying ourselves physically and conceptually in the social world as it is itself unfolding before us. This means that we are never merely "there," present in the world; or, better still, "being merely there" is itself a particular mode of practical being. We are always open to the world, receiving it into ourselves, and equally giving of ourselves to the world, deploying ourselves such that the world is always interactively receiving us into it. Practice is how we come to belong to the world, and how we come to see the world as belonging to us.[18] It is important to note that at the same time as it highlights this unfolding as an ongoing spatial transaction, practice also underscores the unfolding of social being in time.

This interest in time is an important part of Bourdieu's intellectual history. His philosophy thesis, supervised by Georges Canguilhem, aimed at developing the Heideggerian and Husserlian problematic of the temporal dimensions of being insofar as it concerns affective life.[19] In it Bourdieu sought to pursue the phenomenological quest of capturing human existence as it unfolds *in* time rather than *against* time. This was later to form a core Heideggerian problematic: Time haunts philosophical theories of being, but only to be negated.[20] It starts with Parmenides's notion of being as that which is always present, to the more explicit Augustinian formulation of being as that which escapes time, and all the way to the

Cartesian *cogito* and Kantian a priori. Martin Heidegger's answer, which was already embryonically present in Edmund Husserl, is that this was a form of avoidance, of "bad faith," Sartre would later say—a refusal to face up to the limited temporality of being. That is why, for Heidegger, *Dasein* came to mean not only "Here is being," in the classical Heideggerian sense of "Here is where the question of being is raised," but also, as the meaning of *da sein* equally intimates, "Here is what is about to pass, what is here only for a short time—a desperately brief amount of time," Heidegger would say, but a being that nonetheless evolves in and with time and not against it.

As is well known, while in Algeria, Bourdieu turned away from phi- losophy as a career choice and embraced anthropology. And when *habitus* makes its appearance in his early Algerian writings, it can be seen that the question he had posed for himself in his philosophy thesis had clearly remained an important one for him in his ethnographic investigations. Indeed, with habitus, Bourdieu draws on his philosophical investigation of time to conceive of his practical agent as constituted *in time* (that is, historically), deploying itself *in time* (the temporality of the unfolding of practices), and playing *with time* (i.e., making strategic use of time).[21] Such a conception offers a clearly different perspective on the social world to a structuralist approach that ironed out the temporal unfolding of life. It is not an accident that Bourdieu's theory of practice takes its first explicit form in the critique of the then-dominant structuralist conception of gift exchange that epitomized this atemporal analytics. For Bourdieu, the conception of gift exchange as a total operation that synchronically compresses giving, taking, and giving back highlighted the insufficiency of structuralist analysis.[22] How can one develop an understanding of gift exchange while leaving out the question of temporality? It is not that gift exchange unfolds in time just like any other practice. It is more that the playing with time— knowing *when* to give, take, and give back—is the essence of the gift.[23] As I have already noted, I have never come to understand Bourdieu's theory of practice as being "in competition" with the insights of a structuralist approach. I see it as offering a different important perspective that yields many analytical gains, but gains that can easily be seen as complementary rather than in opposition to structuralism, even if the two approaches entail radically different modes of seeing the social world. Still, there is no doubt that structuralism, with its synchronic assumptions, is not suited for an understanding of the intricate relation between gift exchange and time.

In his conception of the practices involved in gift exchange, Bourdieu places great importance on the idea that to engage in a satisfactory way in gift exchange necessitates a lot more than knowing its "rules." It requires a kind of social dexterity that presupposes several temporal, spatial, and social practical skills. First, it entails various degrees of sensitivity and perspicacity when reading the total social scene where a gift offering is being made: Given that every minor aspect of what is being given, where it is given, and how it is given matters, one's sophistication in reading an offering affects one's ability to give back appropriately. Second, it involves degrees of deftness, adroitness, and inventiveness necessary for knowing and being able to act on the knowledge of what, where, and when to give back. In giving back, social agents want to do more than just satisfy "the rule of giving back." They usually want to send a positive or negative message to the person who initiated the exchange. Indeed, not wanting to send a message is a message in itself. Third, it involves degrees of effortlessness and smoothness in carrying out the acts. Ideally, their efficient manner of execution is accompanied by a sense of gracefulness and ease.

It can be said that the three types of capabilities and dimensions of practice just mentioned—perspicacity, efficiency, and smoothness—are at the core of Bourdieu's conception of practical viability. As important, these capabilities are not equally possessed among the members of a social group. Some are virtuosos of gift exchange and some less so. Some feel totally at home in the world of the gift and some less so. Some do the right thing effortlessly and some less so. For Bourdieu these differences in capacities, social ease, and energy expenditure while performing a task have to do with the social agents' different social locations and histories, particularly the different histories of social habituation. The more people are endowed with such practical abilities, the more they can augment their being through the practices they deploy. Habitus is a social scientific theorization of the social agents that allows one to account best for these differences in the capacity to generate viable practices, to unfold efficiently into the world as the world is unfolding before us. I will use an ethnographic case study to highlight the Bourdieusian problematic that is of importance to us here.

On Diasporic Fatigue

If you have researched, or perhaps simply if you have come to know, recently arrived immigrants from rural milieus who have settled in a new city, you will be familiar with the phenomenon that I am about to describe here, and which can be referred to as diasporic fatigue.

Following a period where exhilaration at being in a new place fades and reality sets in, an observer cannot fail to notice how often a sentiment and a discourse of "tiredness" becomes integral to the process of settling into the new environment. It is expressed by a marked rise in the number of situations and occasions where immigrants explicitly say that they are feeling tired, drained, and exhausted. It is also conveyed by a multiplicity of expressions that denote a prolonged state of fatigue accompanied by various modes of repetitive sighing, groaning, and moaning.

There is no doubt that this diasporic fatigue can be one of the psychological effects of leaving one's family and friends and the place that one has grown up in. Yet if one accompanies and observes such newly settled immigrants on their newly acquired daily routines, such as going to work, reporting to a government office, or even shopping, another phenomenon comes to the fore: Each and every mundane task they must perform demands a level of mental and physical energy expenditure, an amount of time, and a degree of concentration that is way beyond what is demanded of long-term inhabitants performing a similar task.

Take something as simple as catching a bus. It involves getting out the door; working out every step of the way to get to the bus stop; asking oneself—or, worse, having to ask strangers—whether one is taking the right turn (and living with the anxiety of not knowing whether one has made the right decision); working out which bus stop one needs to wait at, and on which side of the street; how to board a bus, how to pay, how to insert a card, where to sit; and being anxious about not missing where to get off. All this is without considering the difficulties associated with not knowing the language well enough, if that happens to be the case, but also not knowing the culturally accepted modes of interaction—not knowing how to read people's facial approvals or disapprovals of what one is doing. What's more, even when one learns to do one thing or another, one needs to continually adapt to different circumstances: what to do if it's pouring rain, what to do when the pedestrian crossing is blocked, where to walk when it is overly hot, what to do when one has overslept and needs to rush, and so on. The difficulties are many, and listing them can take a long time.

Bourdieu likes to think that this is how the social world will end up if one follows through the implications of rational choice or any other voluntaristic theory of social action: inhabited by people continuously asking themselves what is the best, proper, optimal (i.e., rational) thing to do here or there, as if at every moment of one's life one is encountering a novel situation. This would not only make for a lot of tired people but also—and notably—for an impossibly dysfunctional society: Imagine how smooth a bus trip would be if every passenger who hops on the bus is deliberating about whether and where to insert the bus card, where to go, and where to stop; if every bus driver is deliberating about where to turn; and if every other motorist in the street is sitting there wondering which way to turn. Indeed, imagine a city full of newly arrived people who cannot rely on a familiarity with its space, its practices, its explicit rules, and so on. It is not just the customers who are newly arrived immigrants but also the workers, the people offering you services. It goes without saying that such a city is unimaginable. As Bourdieu puts it, "[the] world needs to be regular" for it to be a social world.[24] Indeed, one doubts whether "rational choice theorists" are as bad as Bourdieu makes them out to be such as to think of society in the way described above.

The Social and the Habitual

One of the first things highlighted by the problematic of diasporic fatigue, as presented above, is the importance of routinized practices for the very existence of society. The viability of a city or of any inhabited social space, its very ability to exist and to reproduce itself, is dependent on a significant number of its inhabitants being either born and raised in it or having lived in it long enough—enough, that is, to have become intimately acquainted with its physical, social, and cultural environments, such that a large proportion of their everyday practices are done in a relatively effortless, routinized, and efficient habitual manner.

This point might sound banal and obvious. Yet it is important. Indeed, it has been made by many past sociologists and anthropologists such as Franz Boas, Émile Durkheim, Edward Burnett Tylor, and Max Weber when speaking of habits and customs, despite the many differences among them.[25] It has also been made by classical theorists of everyday life, such as Henri Lefebvre, who have reflected on habits and customs.[26] Societies and cultures are not something occasional. There is no social without a continuity in the physical and symbolic infrastructures of society, in the social relations of power and domination, and in cultural practices, among many other things. This continuity, and thus society itself, is achieved through the existence of these habituated practices.[27] *Habitual practices and the habituated social agents that perform them are the very stuff with which and from which the social is made.* They are a necessary and essential, even if not a sufficient, component in the making of the social. *Essential* would not convey fully what is being said here if we are to understand it as a matter of external causality, such as, "It is essential to be tall to be able to see this view." Rather, *essential* must be understood as meaning a "necessary constitutive part."

If, from a diachronic perspective, one can conceive of social agents as separate from society, in that people are born into a preexisting social order and come to internalize it, then from a synchronic perspective that social order always already comprises the individuals who are reproducing it through their routinized practices. We get a hint here of the difficulty that makes the differentiation between structure and agency always destined to miss the mark. If the diachronic perspective allows for thinking about structure and agency, society, and socialized individuals as another chicken-and-egg problematic, this is not possible from a synchronic perspective. For here there are no metaphoric chickens and eggs. Society and the social agents engaging in routinized practices are not external to each other. Society is impossible to conceive without these habituated bodies since they are part of its very makeup. Asking what comes first, society or social agents with habituated bodies, is as absurd as asking which comes first, the chicken or its bodily parts. The social agents and their practices that Bourdieu aims to capture analytically with habitus are social in both the diachronic and the synchronic senses. Diachronically, they are inheritors of the societies and, more particularly, the social locations, they are born into; synchronically, through their routinized practices, they are one of the constitutive elements that make up the social world. They make the social world just as much as they are made by it.

It is crucial to remember the Durkheimian tradition to which the conception of social practices described above belongs. Given that the word *social* can denote many different things with very different ramifications, to emphasize the Durkheimian inheritance that is present in the Bourdieusian usage of the term is to emphasize that *social* refers to something that pertains to an order of facts—that is, an order of reality that is separate and different from the order of reality of the individuals that make it up.[28] Social practices are part of what is referred to as *social reality*; the term aims to convey the idea that the social is real, *sui generis*; it has its own reality, irreducible to the reality of its individual components.[29] It can be said that persons and groups have a dimension that highlights their individuality (or, in the latter case, the individuality of their members), and they have a dimension that is social, ensnared in social institutions and social relations that have, in a way, "captured" them.[30] Bourdieu's habitus is interested in that dimension before all else. It aims to theorize social agents and the routinized practices they engage in insofar as they are social facts. It is not a theory of *individuals* insofar as they are bodies detached from society.

The importance of this Bourdieusian/Durkheimian differentiation between individual and social practices comes to the fore in many discussions of "habit" that fail to differentiate between individual and social habits. It is not that the two are unrelated, but there are clear dimensions of social habits that are not touched on by approaches that are not concerned with the social. Neuroscientific and certain psychological approaches, for instance, are solely interested in habits insofar as they constitute a particular state of the body. They highlight relations and transformations within the habituated body, such as the relations between the brain, the nervous system, and the muscles.[31] These modes of acquiring bodily knowledge are clearly important for any understanding of habit, social or otherwise. Nonetheless, some classical examples of habitual reflexes or of individual habits—such as the person who habitually puts on their left sock before their right sock in the morning, or the person who uses their right hand rather than their left hand when they sneeze—are useful for an understanding of the habituation of the individual body but lack what is one of the most important dimensions that make a practice social: They barely constitute a relation with the social. Discussions about habit where the emphasis is largely on the state of habituated minds and bodies direct analytical attention away from the manner in which social habits constitute particular ways of being enmeshed in the social world. Yet it is precisely this enmeshment, not just the state of the body, that is of interest to social science.

John Dewey's conception of habit, which Bourdieu has looked at favorably,[32] makes this point clear. As Tony Bennett has pointed out, Dewey does not see habits as "belonging exclusively to a self . . . isolated from natural and social surroundings." Rather, he sees them as "working adaptations of personal capacities with environing forces."[33] It is precisely this conception of social/habituated practices as practices that are well-adapted to the social world that Bourdieu's habitus is primarily concerned with. A further important dimension of Dewey's idea of habit that prefigures Bourdieu's is that it is a form of practice that is constitutive of one's social surroundings, not merely something constituted in it. As Michael Halewood notes, for Dewey, "Habits and dispositions comprise 'positive forms of action' which require an external environment. . . . They are 'adjustments *of* the environment, not merely *to* it.'"[34]

Habitual Practices and Social Viability

I have so far used some of the features of *diasporic fatigue*, as described above, to highlight the way the social and the habituated go hand in hand. Habituated social agents are an integral part of the making of society. Through their habitual practices, they make up and inhabit the social world by practically relating to it in a particular way. One needs to always think of habit specifically as a habitual way of inhabiting the social world to ensure one does not forget this relational dimension. There is another, obvious but important, point brought to the fore by the phenomenon of diasporic fatigue: Habituated practices are essential for the well-being of the social agents themselves; such practices stop them from becoming fatigued. The more habituated one is, the less tired one is. Like Maurice Merleau-Ponty's famous examples regarding typists and musicians, if a person is typing a word or playing a note on a musical instrument, they stop thinking about which finger they ought to use and how to move that finger to reach a specific letter, or press a key or a hole to play a note; but if they think about the letters or the notes in such a conscious manner, they will stop typing or playing music efficiently and smoothly.[35] Lack of conscious knowledge and the acquisition of bodily knowledge through habituation and sedimentation are not only important and good but also *necessary* for a fulfilling life. In a different but equally important way, Frantz Fanon describes very well how the racist gaze that makes the racialized person overly conscious of their body destroys the bodily schema and its balancing effect on the person.[36] The racist gaze destroys the body's implicit integrity and its sense of spatial orientation, which now becomes possible only through a conscious effort. This stands in opposition to the experience of the spatiality of the body as highlighted by Merleau-Ponty when describing our capacity to pass through a door without having measured the width of the door.[37] An overly conscious sense of the spatiality of the body is debilitating, even if it succeeds in keeping the body together, as in the case of many racialized people. This is all to say that the fatigue of the nonhabituated person is not only physical but affective, psychological, and cognitive. Without the embodied knowledge and affective confidence of habitual practices, social life would be exhausting and unviable in the long term. It is because of this that the ability to produce habituated practices, to inhabit the world habitually is intimately related to people's well-being.

Here social being and social viability are primarily associated with this sense of affinity and intimacy with—and adequacy in the face of—the flow of the social world: How adequate do we feel in the face of what society throws in our face? How well can we anticipate how it unfolds before us? How efficient are we in performing the tasks we set out to perform? How at ease do we feel performing them? How satisfied are we by what we are performing? Society distributes these capacities for adequacy, efficiency, homeliness, and practical satisfaction unequally. Social agents often receive them diachronically in the form of internalized inheritances whose value they try to maintain or augment. But it is important to reiterate that efficiency, adequacy, and a sense of homeliness are not merely individual capacities, since they implicate the social agent's relations with their social context. The struggle to keep them valuable is intimately bound with the reproduction of the contexts in which they are viable.

From such a perspective, social agents thrive when their capacity to execute the practical tasks they are confronted with is as good as can be, when the environment in which they are deploying themselves is as suited to them as possible, and when the tasks they are actually performing are as rewarding as can be. It is an inherent dimension of the social agents' practical being to struggle for a coupling of efficiency and effortlessness that is as close as possible. But they do so according to the way they have internalized—through repetition, habituation, and sedimentation— certain historically and situationally acquired capacities. Habitus is a social scientific conception, a theory, of this historically acquired practical efficiency-generating dimension of social agents.

To fully understand this relation between habitual inhabitance of the world and social viability, something important regarding diasporic fatigue needs to be stressed: at the opposite end of the spectrum to the newly arrived migrant body, for whom every situation is a case of "first contact," is not an automaton who does things mechanically in a robotic fashion, but someone who has repeated the same habitual practice differently in many different circumstances and has thus developed a sense of what to do even when confronted with a vast array of new circumstances. Despite every major theorist of habit aiming to highlight the importance of this creative dimension that is inherent to practice, and despite its common-sense obviousness to anyone reflecting on their own habits, we still have a tradition of thinking about habits that equates them to the robotic repetition of the same. Social habits, at the very least, are never of that order. In the way one comes to better understand a word and when to use it by encountering it in a multiplicity of contexts (at least as a Wittgensteinian approach would have it[38]), the habituated body is a body that has engaged in the same routine in a multiplicity of contexts and has thus developed a certain intimacy with the range of possibilities one has at hand in the moment of an encounter with a specific situation.

Furthermore, for Bourdieu, the social is imagined not only spatially but also as a temporal flow. These everyday changes encountered in routinized practices are not just spatial events. Society does not merely put social agents in particular locations; it positions them vis-à-vis a life that is unfolding before them. There are events and happenings that are continuously heading toward them, as it were, and that they have to foresee and anticipate.[39] Consequently, a habituated practice, based on the past experiences of the habituated subject, incorporates a capacity to anticipate the immediate future that is already unfolding in the present. Bourdieu and others have used many sports metaphors to highlight the way—propelled by past experiences—that social subjects are able to confront the unfolding future coming toward them.[40] None have used what I feel the most apt sport in thinking about this situation: surfing, because a wave is the product of water coming from two opposite directions. Like social agents propelled by their history as a force coming from behind them and facing the future as a force coming toward them, the surfer is also propelled by water coming from behind them while facing a flow of water coming toward them. I feel that thinking about the surfer in this way is at the very least a good way of imagining the positioning of the social agent in time as far as Bourdieu is concerned.

To speak of routinized practices in society is to speak of the capacity to maintain a routine under very different circumstances by continually adjusting it to new states of the self and new happenings. Being habituated to take the bus to work means knowing how to take it in many different circumstances and different states of the self and being able to anticipate certain happenings that will unfold in different unforeseen situations. One does not need to have read Gilles Deleuze to know that a practice can never be the same when it is being repeated. If nothing else, one is at least a few minutes older and has benefited from a certain past that has just been experienced. As with Bourdieu's analysis of gift exchange as a practice, the habituated person heading to work, as opposed to the newly arrived immigrant, is someone who possesses what we can refer to as various degrees of temporal, spatial, and social sensitivity and perspicacity needed for reading the total social scene before them; who has degrees of deftness, adroitness, and inventiveness in the handling of unforeseen situations, as when they wake up late, when the bus is late, or when the bus route has been changed because of some roadwork; and, last but not least, who is in possession of degrees of effortlessness and efficiency in carrying out the foregoing. As I have already noted, it is the capacity of the habituated mind-body assemblage to generate practices that aim to augment being through the maximization of this perspicacity, efficiency, and effortlessness that Bourdieu's habitus aims to capture. Consequently, it is useful to go further into what each entails—keeping in mind that for Bourdieu, each represents not simply a capacity of the habituated mind-body assemblage but a relation to the social world.

Toward a Political Economy of Symbolic, Practical, and Affective Collusion

Highlighting perspicacity as a dimension of habitual practices is already important in pointing to a mistaken assumption that one often makes when speaking of habit. Wanting to highlight the way habit involves less *mental deliberation* and more *body knowledge*, as we have done already, one easily slips into mind-body dualism, whereby habits are imagined as more body than mind. In the process it is often forgotten that habits also involve habits of the mind. This is why I have been using the term *mind-body assemblage* to try to minimize this tendency to forget that our classification and categories and modes of thinking and knowing are themselves more or less habitual. Perspicacity situates us into this dimension of habituated practices.

The Microsoft Word thesaurus I am using as I write this text gives us such synonyms of *perspicacity* as: *acuity*, *perceptiveness*, and *insightfulness*. These are useful in pointing to what a perspicacious practice means: it is a practice in which the agent is able to "read" the world unfolding before them in a sharp and clear-sighted manner. The more perspicacious social agents are, the better they are at reading the reality around them, and the sharper and subtler the concepts, categories, and classifications they have for understanding the world around them. The same thesaurus, however, also takes us to such synonyms as *cleverness* and *intelligence*. This makes it seem as if this sharp ability to capture what is happening around us is a matter of innate brainpower of some sort. For Bourdieu this is the source of an error made not only by laypeople but by more specialized professional thinkers dealing with this matter: a naturalization of the objects of the world and the categories we have at our disposal to understand them.[41] In *Outline of a Theory of Practice* Bourdieu is already admonishing phenomenologists for doing just this: When they claim to want to study things "as they are," they take the adequacy of people's categories about the world for granted.[42] It is as if the adequacy and, indeed, perspicacity, of the categories we have at our disposal to see and understand the world is something unproblematic, something that goes without saying.

Instead Bourdieu wants to highlight that this perspicacity is a historical process where both the categories of perception and the perceived realities that the categories are signifying are born and evolve in close relation to each other.[43] This mutual shaping is what gives a habituated knowledge a particular form, hinted at in one of the French words used to signify knowledge: *connaissance*. To any French-speaking person, *connaissance* immediately alludes to *co-naissance*, which literally means "cobirth." Many take it to be the etymology of the word, though it is not. Still, the allusion to a relation between "knowing" and "being born with the object of knowledge" has been taken up by many. As with Merleau-Ponty's deployment of *connaître* to highlight that knowledge comes not only from being born "in the world" but from being "born with the world,"[44] Bourdieu also deploys it to allude to a knowledge born out of a historical relation of coemergence, coevolution, and coaffinity.[45] In this ideal knowledge situation, the complicity between habitual practice and the social reality it is enmeshed in is not only historical but *genetic*, in the sense of having the same genesis. It begins the moment that both the practice and the surrounding reality come into existence and give birth to each other. This points to what is perhaps the most important dimension of not only habitual perspicacious classification but habitual practices in general, as far as Bourdieu is concerned. There is in habitual practice what we might call an ontological affinity and collusion between the mind-body assemblage and the environment in which that body is practically enmeshed. It is in this relation of complicity and connivance that the habitual and the augmentation of being become articulated. Social agents augment their being most when they are deploying themselves in the very environment that has created them and that they have created. This ontological complicity is what also defines the efficiency and effortlessness that further characterize habituated practices.

What does it mean to speak of the efficiency of the practicing agent? For Bourdieu, this is primarily about the efficiency of the mind to think about, categorize, and apprehend the world adequately, and the efficiency of the body in deploying itself and performing effectively whatever task it is engaging in. Because of their interest in the power of the performativity of language, Judith Butler is one of the few to highlight the questions of "efficacity" in Bourdieu, but they reduce what Bourdieu is saying to something like the following: efficacity (in their language, "performatives that work") equals legitimacy equals degree of power. As Butler puts it, "For Bourdieu, then, the distinction between performatives that work and those that fail has everything to do with the social power of the one who speaks: the one who is invested with legitimate power makes language act; the one who is not invested may recite the same formula, but produces no effects. The former is legitimate, and the latter, an imposter."[46] In this way, Butler elides an important difference between efficacity and efficiency. Basic writing dictionaries warn against conflating effectiveness and efficacy, on the one hand, and efficiency, on the other. Effectiveness and efficacy have to do with the body having the adequate capacity to perform a task, while efficiency involves the further dimension of deploying this effectiveness with a minimum waste of time and effort. In his discussion of habit, William James notes that habits make our expenditure of bodily and mental energy minimal.[47] Clearly the differences between effectiveness/efficacy and efficiency are not either/or matters, for the more capable the body-mind assemblage is, the less expenditure of energy it needs to perform a particular task within a given time. Efficiency necessitates and includes effectiveness/efficacy, but effectiveness does not necessitate and include efficiency. When teaching this difference, I often invite students to pick an ordinary everyday event that has occurred before coming to class and subject it to as minute a description as possible to try and see how the question of efficiency can be captured ethnographically. I will do the same here by choosing a mundane situation I was in before writing this version of my text.

I am sitting in my lounge room discussing potential renovations with a tradesperson who's never been to my house before. My partner is heading out of the house and says, "I've left you two cups of tea on the kitchen table." I invite the tradesperson to come with me to the kitchen table to pick up the cups of tea. Mundane as it might be, carrying out this task entails a number of cognitive and physical operations. How *efficiently* the task is performed will depend on the mental, physical, and affective capabilities of my and the tradesperson's mind-body assemblage. These are partly biological, but, as with the example of the newly arrived migrants above, they are also dependent on certain sedimented histories of performative familiarities (acquaintance with what needs to be done) and environmental familiarities (a sense of belonging or at least an acquaintance with the situational context where the task is done).

Because this is my house, I have often gone to pick up a cup of tea from the kitchen table. Unlike the tradesperson, I don't need to strain myself to know where the kitchen is or how to get to it from the lounge room. Nor do I need to strain myself to know where the kitchen table is in the kitchen. Furthermore, unlike the tradesperson, I have often used the mugs that my partner left on the table and have no problem recognizing them. Thus, I will spend much less energy than my guest, who will be asking themself where the kitchen is, where the kitchen table is, which cup on the table they should pick up, and so on. Here, efficiency is straightforwardly affected by degrees of practical familiarity and an internalized history of repetition. Nonetheless, the advantages we are speaking of in this context are very minor. Most bodies can rely on, and will benefit from, a history of performing similarly structured movements, even if in a different environment.

The tradesperson might be a Turkish coffee drinker, with their hand and fingers more inclined to hold the smaller coffee cups used for Turkish coffee. Clearly, such differences and the effects of those differences are again likely to be infinitely minimal. But this does not mean that they are nonexistent. By trying to hold a mug the tradesperson might be performing a practice that goes against their inclination and, as such, the task will involve more hesitancy and will require more mental and physical energy. Note that here the notion of *inclination* relates to both physiological and psychological dimensions of practice. Psychologically, my guest might be, in terms of their desires, "inclined" to drink coffee and is only agreeing to drink tea out of politeness. This kind of inclination does indeed affect the efficiency of the act. As we shall later see, it is where the order of the *illusio* and that of the habitus meet. But habitus, as we shall also see in chapter 2, is also concerned with the inclination of the body as such. The latter is a more physical inclination denoting the way body muscles have been shaped by their practically mediated social history. Here, inclination is physiological—or even, simply, physical—in the way certain trees by the beach acquire an inclination through a history of exposure to winds coming from a particular direction.

The tradesperson might also be slowed down by being less at ease, and generally under more affective strain, because they are a stranger to the household. This brings in the dimension of smoothness. From this angle, efficiency and smoothness are affected by one's sense of belonging, which is a version of the relation of collusion highlighted above. The homely confidence that marks my demeanor as opposed to the tradesperson's is a direct product of the historical collusion that exists between my home and myself. This confidence not only reproduces my sense of belonging but also the relation between us as a relation of insider and outsider. The tradesperson might spill a bit of tea, and I can tell them not to worry. It is unthinkable that they would tell me not to worry. By saying "Don't worry," I am putting them at ease, but I am affirming my position as the one who belongs and decides what one should worry about in this space.

Still, my sense of belonging can take me only as far as efficiency goes. The tradesperson might go to the gym every day and be fitter than I am, and, as such, even for such a simple and easy task that requires very little effort, might be more *efficacious* at picking up the cup from the table once they have located it. Efficacy is not efficiency, but it helps. The tradesperson is also younger and more mentally alert. The mind-body assemblage (particularly the eyes) must unconsciously "know" the distance between one's body and where the cup is located. It must estimate the weight of the cup of tea, think about heat, and evaluate where to grab the cup. This is all performed without much explicit calculation, in a way similar to Merleau-Ponty's description of the body going through the door. The body (the shoulder, the upper arm, the lower arm, and the hand) deploys itself accordingly to grab the cup. It must also grab the cup of tea with minimal trembling so as not to spill the contents on the way back to the lounge. Given their youth and fitness, the tradesperson might be more efficacious in this regard. So maybe the spilled tea was caused by nervousness. Over the years, it is I who has furnished this kitchen. I have bought a table that suits my height. I have positioned everything in my house in a way that suits me best. I am not only adjusted to this homely environment but have struggled as much as I can, ever since I've lived in this house, to ensure that this environment is adjusted to me. Once again we see how efficiency relates to degrees of adequation and collusion that exist between practical agents and the environment in which they are deploying themselves.

Smoothness might appear no different from efficiency, and to some extent it is no different. It nonetheless involves pushing further the collusion, complicity, and affinity that mark habituated practices. Perhaps this can be conveyed using Bourdieu's beloved tennis metaphors: The tennis player returned what was a very powerful serve efficiently and, what's more, it was done so smoothly that they made it look effortless. Habitual practices that convey effortlessness and smoothness convey a certain grace on top of efficiency. Merleau-Ponty, describing the way we appropriate and "fuse" with some of the objects that surround us, speaks of "the power we have of dilating our being in the world."[48] It can be said that the degrees to which habituated practices are perspicacious, efficient, effortless, and smooth reflect degrees of dilation into the social world as a whole.

There would be many other factors and issues to consider if we were to aim for a fuller analysis of all that is involved in the multiplicity of moves that walking to the kitchen table and picking up the cup of tea calls for. Had my guest been a non-English speaker or simply from a region with a very different English accent, we could have started our analysis earlier with the differential capacity to understand what my partner said when they said, "I've left you two cups of tea on the kitchen table." And we have barely touched on the culture of tea drinking and the ethnic, class, and gender differences that can affect the practice of picking up a cup of tea. These add to the strain of picking up the cup—the stress of knowing how to pick it up "properly." We have also barely touched on the cup of tea as an "offering," as a gift to a tradesperson who is about to give us a quote for their commodified labor. Knowing how to accept and how to offer even such a minor gift is of the order of the habitus and has major consequences for how to negotiate our forthcoming transaction. The domains of analysis are probably endless, but what has been mentioned is enough to make it clear that, even in this relatively simple situation, a whole series of differences in efficiency between bodies can be observed: differences in the innumerable things a body finds itself in need of being efficacious at, and differences due to the body's history and its social and cultural location. These are differences in accumulated bodily strength, in bodily know-how, in accumulated belonging, and in spatial familiarity with the environment, among other things.

This takes us to a final point that needs highlighting in our examination of the phenomenon of *diasporic fatigue*: while habituated practices are a necessary dimension of society, not everyone in society is able to engage in routinized habitual practices to the same degree and in the same way. Or, as we can now put it, not everyone is in an equal relation of collusion with the social world and able to draw as much existential fulfillment from deploying themselves practically with it. The example of the newly arrived immigrants provides a sharp contrast to the social agents who are habituated to the world they inhabit. But, as with everything for Bourdieu, what really needs to be captured analytically is that more often than not, degrees of habituation are a matter of more or less rather than either/or. There is no doubt that societies rely for their very existence and reproduction on many social agents engaging in habituated routinized practices. Nonetheless, among those agents who do engage, not everyone is at ease in the same way and to the same degree, and not everyone experiences a sense of fitting in in the same way and to the same degree. Some inherit a sense of being at home in their social space more than others, and some have to work at fostering such a sense of homeliness more than others. By the end of the day, some will end up feeling able to operate in the social world more adequately than others, and these same people will end up reinforcing their sense of belonging, of feeling more "at home" in that social world, more than others. It is this differential that Bourdieu sees as a crucial dimension of his political economy of being.

40   Human bodies, as individuals and assembled as groups—and by virtue of their different practically mediated inheritances, their different practical histories (what the bodies have been subjected to as an imposition or as something sought by the social agent), and their different social and physical locations—are, in any given context, unequally efficient bodies and have unequal relations of intimacy and collusion with the social world they inhabit.

In this chapter, I have been less concerned with habitus as such than with the nature of the social practices that habitus generates and the kind of "being" and "viability" that these practices yield for the social agent that deploys them. I have defined social practices as habituated practices, arguing that they are the very ontological matter from which the social is made. I have argued that these practices yield being and viability to the degree that they are perspicacious, efficient, effortless, and smooth—that is, through the degrees of symbolic, affective, and practical collusion they have with the world that is unfolding around them. Here social being and social viability are primarily associated with a sense of affinity, intimacy, and adequacy in the face of the flow of social world: How well do we feel able to read the world around us? How adequate do we feel in the face of what society throws in our face? How efficient are we in performing the tasks we set out to perform? How at ease do we feel performing them? Society distributes these capacities for augmenting our being through developing these senses of adequacy, efficiency, homeliness, and practical satisfaction unequally. Social agents receive these capacities diachronically in the form of internalized inheritances, whose value they try to maintain or augment. In chapter 2 we will examine habitus as the very mechanism responsible for the generation of such practical modes of augmenting one's being.

Structure, Capacity, and Dispositionality

2

In chapter 1, I highlighted the correlation between the degree of habituation of practices and the extent to which they are in collusion with the environment in which they are being deployed. The greater the collusion, the greater the perspicacity, efficiency, and smoothness necessary for the social agents' accumulation of being. Since routinized events and repetitive happenings are never absolutely the same, practices never repeat exactly what they are repeating, either.[1] There are always variations. Habituation means being able to reconsider, change, and adjust one's mode of deployment when encountering such variations with minimal mental and physical exertion. I also insisted on the productive nature of these practices. They are continuously aiming to make the environment suit them just as they are aiming to make themselves best suited for that environment. In that sense we can say that they are in a continuous state of coattunement with the environments in which they are generated, continuously attuning themselves to a changing environment while making the environment attuned to them. As most definitions of habitus highlight, it is a concept that tries to capture the different ways the body-mind assemblage sediments past habitual experiences and becomes the site for the generation of these practices of coattunement.

Habitus Between Reproduction and Social Change

As I also pointed out in chapter 1, for Pierre Bourdieu, to say that practices are habitual and to say that they are social is one and the same thing. Habituated practices and the social world are not occasional happenings. They have an inherent capacity to maintain themselves over long periods of time.[2] And this is so despite all the changes. That a set of social relations and practices remains the same amid a state of continual change is part of what makes them social. It can easily be said that despite all the ongoing transformations that Western European societies have experienced and continue to experience, say, over the last one hundred years, the reproduction of the core social relations of capitalism, patriarchy, and colonial racism that are at their core has continued unabated. Despite years of celebrating how Western societies allow people to experience "upward social mobility," the reproduction of class positions across generations continues to outweigh such mobility. Despite laws against discrimination and major changes in attitude, relations of patriarchal and colonial power still mark workplaces in assigning who can do what and who can climb to management positions.

It is in this sense that, for Bourdieu, being interested in social reality means, by definition, to be interested in a reality that has a certain degree of structural consistency, constancy, and synchronicity over time.[3] For him, saying that one is not interested in studying reproduction is akin to saying one is not interested in studying social phenomena tout court. Yet, as far as Bourdieu is concerned, reproduction is far from being uninteresting and predictable and is of the order of the incredible and even the magical. The magic lies precisely in the fact that the core structures of society continue to be reproduced even though social life at a certain level is indeed continually changing. It is so precisely because social agents are more than mere support for social relations.[4] The magic lies also in the fact that the core structures of society are reproduced even though agents experience volition and spontaneity and act creatively in the face of continuously new situations. For Bourdieu, something as banal and taken for granted as people continuing to speak the same language they have spoken the day before, the same language they spoke years before, the same language their parents and grandparents spoke before them—even though people continually live through new linguistic realities—is nothing short of extraordinary.

Rather than creating an opposition between continuity and social change or between the work of reproduction and the experience of volition, spontaneity, and creativity in a forever transforming social world, the task is to show how this creativity is part of the process of reproduction rather than its opposite. This is what habitus aims to explain. It is a theorization of the body-mind assemblage's capacity to be structured and spontaneous or reproductive and creative at the same time. As to spontaneity and volition that is not reproductive of the core structures of society, this is a possibility for Bourdieu, as we shall later see, but one that can only be wrested from the social rather than taken as something that is pedestrianly available, as some who are after a sociology of "social change" claim.[5]

Social agents internalize the social world they live in, and this internalization gives them a differential capacity to fit into the world, to generate more or less efficient practices, and to experience a greater or lesser sense of belonging.[6] Habitus is a theory of what social subjects, as mind-body assemblages, are made from, such that they can be the scene of these processes of historical internalization and generalization. In doing so habitus illustrates, more than any other category, the work that Bourdieu expects a theoretical category to do. This is particularly so in the way it is made to perform a triple act that seems at first sight contradictory. It is made to capture practical being first, from the inside, as it is lived by the agent, and second, from the outside in terms of its relation to its micro- and macroconstitutive elements as they are experienced by the social analyst. Third, it embodies a reflection on its very nature as a theoretical concept produced from a social scientific position. It is spoken of with an experiential phenomenological language of "sense of practice," "flair," "know-how," and "bodily knowledge" and with the analytical language of structuralism, as in the famed "structured structures (that are) structuring structures."[7] Then we also have the language of "inclination," "dispositions," and "capacities" that, as we shall see, mediates between the two levels. We shall now delve into what kind of theory habitus is. But, before doing so, a word about the choice of the term itself.

Bourdieu is hardly the first to think through this repetitive-but-creative dimension of practical being.[8] Nor is he the first to use *habitus* or other words derived from *habit* (*habitude* in French) to refer to it. Some ancient philosophers used the terms *habit*, *habitude*, and their equivalents, though the terms were less common and more of a "learned" concept at the time.[9]

Maurice Merleau-Ponty favored the term *habitude*, while Edmund Husserl preferred the term *habitus*.[10] Largely speaking, though, they were grappling with the same problems and the term they used, whether *habitus* or *habitude*, was doing the same work. With Pierre Bourdieu, one can say that his choice of *habitus* is not so arbitrary, even if he most likely inherited it directly from Husserl while investigating the latter's conceptions of time for his doctoral dissertation. Unlike Husserl or Merleau-Ponty, Bourdieu wrote sociology and philosophy not only for sociologists and philosophers but as a mode of public intervention.[11] This is an important difference. Husserl and Merleau-Ponty were inaccessible to the layperson, but the layperson was not in their field of vision as they spoke and wrote. Bourdieu, like Jean-Paul Sartre in this regard, faced a more difficult task. For, while wanting his writings and his concepts to be taken seriously by other social scientists and philosophers as original contributions to his field of scholarship, he simultaneously wrote with laypeople in mind. This was and still is a difficult task for an academic to perform.

As noted in the introduction to this book, Bourdieu wanted his concepts to participate in the political economy of being that he was delineating. He hoped that the communication of his concepts to laypeople could help them in their struggle to augment their being. In choosing habitus he was telling readers that it is related to habit but also more than habit; that it conveys something more difficult than what the concept of habit conveys; and that if they bothered to think about it, they might gain some helpful insights into their lives.

Habitus as a Theory of What We Are

To highlight that habitus is a theory is to say that it is produced by theorists for the purpose of better understanding and explaining the reality that is being theorized. This reality is us, human beings, insofar as we are social beings—"practicing social agents." Throughout this chapter we will deal with the complexities of what a theory is for Bourdieu and how it works, but at this stage it is important to begin by emphasizing one crucial point to help direct the reader's imaginary as this chapter unfolds. This point has to do with the significance of the *are* when we speak of habitus as a theory of what practicing social agents *are*. It is common to talk about habitus in terms of something we *have*. This is not entirely false in that in everyday parlance *to be* and *to have* are often used interchangeably. We say we *have* "healthy genes," even though our genes are part of what we *are* rather than something that we have. This wouldn't matter if it wasn't for the fact that, in general, *having* denotes a certain distance and a relation of exteriority between subject and object, such as when we say "I have a pen." To understand habitus it is important to avoid thinking of it in this way. If it is spoken of as a theory of something that we have, it can only be so as far as it is technically a theory of what we are. It is a theory of our *inner social constitution*, as it were. Because of this complexity, understanding the differentiation and the relation between *to have* and *to be* is crucial for taking habitus both as a theory of the nature of the social agent and as a generative mechanism.

It is agreed that the dominant philosophical usage of the concept of habitus comes from Thomas Aquinas, who uses Boethius's translation of *hexis*, Aristotle's concept that Husserl, and Bourdieu after him, continued to use along with *habitus*.[12] Aristotle's *hexis* already contained the core dimensions of what came to characterize habitus for Aquinas and for those after him, including Bourdieu. Most important in relation to what we have been discussing above is the way the notion of *hexis* fuses the notions of "having" and "being."

At its most basic, the verb *to have* today indicates a possession of something and presumably the possession of its capacities. As important, *to have* indicates something that is outside me but that I can have access to and as such enables me. Aristotle channels an exchange in Plato's *Theaetetus* in which Socrates makes this distinction, using the example of "having a coat."[13] For him, a statement such as "I have a coat" tells us that the person making the utterance has access to a coat that is outside them. This gives the person access to its capacities to shield themself from the cold and the rain when necessary. But this does not tell us where the coat is; the person may have it at home, for instance. Consequently, it might well rain and be cold, leaving the person without a coat to shield themself, even though "they have a coat." This kind of having is not the kind of having that Aristotle associates with *hexis*. The kind of having he has in mind is a habitual and ongoing having, whereby what is outside me becomes an inseparable and durable part of me—it becomes me. There is a movement and a fusion between what I have and what I am. *Hexis* is a kind of coat I am always wearing, which allows me always to have not just an abstract capacity, as when I have a coat at home, but the practical capacity to shield myself from the rain and the cold. Never would I have to say I left it at home, because the coat in a sense has become part of me. In fact, it *is* me.

When I have something that is not part of me, that remains outside me, and that I cannot activate at will, Plato and Aristotle refer to this as *ktesis*, in the sense of passive possession.[14] *Hexis* is on the side of active possession or enaction—what Aristotle calls *energeia*.[15] We can see here a dominant trope in the development of habitus: if what I have becomes what I am, it means that what was outside me can become part of me. This expresses the idea that habitus is an "internalization" of past habituated practices that creates in me, through a process of sedimentation, a "durable" mode of being. It is like acquiring "physical fitness" after five years of regular exercise. Fitness becomes a durable quality of my body, something I always have, rather than something I can or cannot have. So it becomes something I am. Habitus, however, is not just general fitness; it is fitness to meet the challenges that a specific social milieu throws at me by the mere fact of living and evolving in it. Because both the body and the space in which the body is immersed are continuously evolving, internalization is a process of coevolution, or what I referred to earlier in the chapter as

Structure, Capacity, and Dispositionality

coattunement. Dispositions are the transformation of the body's capacities such that they become more inclined or geared toward establishing a particular mode of encounter with the social rather than another.

Habitus, unlike an atomic structure of an element, is acquired historically through the internalization and sedimentation of past practices in the body. Still, very much like an atomic structure, it is the structure that *characterizes* the nature of the social agent. A particular habitus defines a particular class of social agents.[16] In turn, an unobservable theorized reality such as habitus reveals itself through the observable modes of appreciation, taste, and behavior, all of which reveal their particularity to the researcher. What links the habitus to the observable behavior is the fact that the latter is a system of dispositions, a generative mechanism, that causes that observable behavior.

A Generative Mechanism, Part 1: An Inner Causal Structure

To be clear, to emphasize that habitus is a *theory* of the efficiency-seeking social agent does not mean that it is *only* an intellectual construct created by analysts to make sense of reality. The emphasis here is on *only*, because, to be sure, it does mean that *also*. Indeed, in choosing a technical word such as *habitus* that is not used in everyday contexts, Bourdieu wants to ensure that we don't forget that it is indeed the product of an intellectual perspective. But the fact that it is an intellectual product does not mean that it only exists for intellectuals. Bourdieu wants to argue that approaching practice in the way he does ensures that the sociologically captured dimension of reality is part of the social agents' reality, even if it is not experienced by the social agent in the same way and with the same language. As such, habitus is a real dimension of the social agent that passively comes forth, or that is actively brought to the fore, through the social analyst's particular perspective and interaction with the agent's mode of experiencing reality. This is easier to accept with respect to the more experiential phenomenological dimension captured by habitus. That is, people are more easily open to accept the idea that they have "inclinations" that they are not aware of. The more analytical conception of habitus as a "structure" is, however, more difficult to digest.

The idea that we *really* "have in us" a mechanism that generates the practices that we deploy in our encounter with the world is less open to common sense. It is of the same order as Sigmund Freud's notion of the unconscious:

an abstract reality that nonetheless comes with the claim of being real. The psychoanalyst will insist that it is there, since it actually generates (it causes) how we think and feel at a more conscious level. Understood in this way, habitus exemplifies Bourdieu's theoretical realism referred to in this book's introduction. Although he never termed it this way, his categories are of the order of what Roy Bhaskar calls the "theoretical real."[17] It is both a theory of the nature and properties and an actual dimension of what it is theorizing. The atomic structure of an element is often used as an example that can help illustrate this. An atomic structure is a theory of the element and a reality accessed by scientists, by virtue of their perspective and their relation to what is being theorized. It is real even if it is not available experientially outside the scientific context. But it is also real through its outward manifestations, such as the way the atomic structure explains certain visible qualities and properties possessed by the element, thereby taking us to the domain of the experiential.

Theoretical real structures, then, are causal structures that help causally explain the manifest dimensions of what they are theorizing. But, as Bhaskar goes to great lengths to explain, they do so with a radically different concept of causality and a radically different conception of explanation than that normalized by positivist science.[18] He argues that positivist causality is temporal: Something is explained by what precedes it and acts on it. Some sociological explanations of what people do are often formulated in this positivist temporal frame: the cause happens at Time 1, to be followed at Time 2 by the reaction it has caused. Whether it is the rationality of the subject or the cultural milieu itself that is seen as the cause, either is conceived as prior to and affecting what the social agent does. In this regard, positivist causality is more in line with the commonsense way in which people articulate what they do and why they do it. Take these two statements: "She stayed with her husband despite his infidelities, because she felt that it would cause her children irreparable psychological damage if she were to leave" and "She stayed with her husband despite his infidelities because leaving was not something either possible or thinkable in the society in which she lived." Even though the two explanations offered here are very different, one operating within a rational choice mode of thinking and the other within a social-deterministic framework, both involve a form of positivist causality where action is explained by what preceded it. In the first case, certain calculations are seen to have been made first, in an attempt to cause the action of "staying with the husband" to happen. In the other, it is the social milieu that preexists the social agent that is seen to determine what the social agent can think or do. Habitus does not work in this way. It also operates with a radically different, critical realist, conception of explanation, which also presumes a different conception of the purpose of scientific inquiry. Here the primary purpose of science is to discover the "properties" of elements and what gives them such properties. While in positivist reasoning being put in the freezer (Time 1) can explain why the water became ice (Time 2), in critical realist reasoning the scientific question is, above all, What is the nature of water, such that when subjected to low temperatures it freezes? This involves investigating the nature of water, which, in turn, becomes an investigation of what gives it its properties, including the property of freezing once subjected to low temperatures. This leads to the investigation of the atomic structure of water necessary to *cause* it to freeze in such conditions.[19] We can see here that the temporal causality—Time 1, placing the water in the freezer, leading to Time 2, water turning to ice—is not negated. But a different scientific gaze, where primacy is given to the search for the generative mechanism that constitutes the nature of the element, is considered more important. From this perspective, the primary causal question has no temporal dimension: What is the nature of water that gives it the property of freezing when subjected to temperatures below zero degrees Celsius?

In much the same way, Bourdieu sees habitus not only as a structure of the socially and historically constructed agent but also as a structure that causes and explains certain of this agent's outward practical manifestations. Habitus, then, is a scientifically captured invisible mechanism that (1) gives us insight into the nature of social agents and (2) that generates the way such social agents manifest themselves in practice. This way of conceiving of habitus is already present, at least implicitly, in some of the earliest usages of the concept. In a well-known piece, François Héran has shown the evolution of habitus as a concept. He traces its presence not only in philosophy but also in early medical language, in which habitus refers to the symptomatic, manifested state of the body in relation to a specific illness affecting it. *Manifested* here means precisely what was alluded to above: an outward appearance generated by an inner state. The word *malade* in French, meaning sick (and whose traces still exist in English in the form of *malady*), has its roots in this usage. It is a contraction of *mal habitus*—a not-so-good outward state of the body generated by some internal state of that body.[20] Here we see the emergence of the idea that the body's visible, outward, symptomatic manifestation in space and time is a product of the inner invisible state of the body. Unlike the atomic structure of an element considered to be its "inherent," "enduring," and "natural" characteristic, the sick state of the body is a fleeting, conjuncturally acquired state. Habitus, in Bourdieu's usage, stands between the two. It is, on the one hand, an environmentally acquired state, with the outside of the body having a long-term effect on shaping the inside; on the other hand, it is a far more durable state than that of an illness. If, by birth, the mind-body is a natural biological being, its evolution in relation to and under the effect of a social milieu makes it a sociobiological being.

A Generative Mechanism, Part 2: Dispositions

The idea that the durable generative mechanism resulting from the sedimentation of habitual practices in the body constitutes a *dispositional* state is another important dimension of *hexis*. It is one that Aristotle had to grapple with and that other theorists after him have continued to try and grapple with. To say, "I am durably this or that" is to say, "I am constantly *disposed* to do this or that." What does it mean to say that I have a bodily disposition and in what way is that different from saying that I have a bodily *capacity*? In an important sense, capacity stands to disposition as *ktesis* stands to *energeia*. To have a capacity to lose my temper when I'm being ticketed for a traffic offense but have no interest in doing so clearly means that losing my temper is something that I *can* do but that I am not *inclined* to do. It is not part of who I am. This is not the same as being disposed to losing my temper when I am being ticketed. There, losing my temper in such situations is something I experience an urge to do. It is part of who I am. What is the difference? One thing is clear, being disposed—experiencing an urge—to losing my temper does not mean that I will necessarily do so. And not being disposed to losing my temper does not mean that I will never do so. In saying that I have a capacity or that I have a disposition to lose my temper, I am saying that I am capable of it. Here lies the difficulty, for neither having a capacity nor having a disposition to do something determines whether I will actually do it. Ancient Greek philosophers spent a lot of time discussing what kind of power this "disposition" is and whether it really exists[21]: How can I say that I have a capacity or a disposition to do something and then not do it? If I am not doing it, what is it exactly that I have? Is it not a bit vague to say that I have a potential, a capacity, or a disposition? What if I have a disposition to lose my temper but in fact never have? How and why would I say that I have such a disposition, and is saying so not a bit meaningless? Why not say that I clearly have a disposition not to lose my temper, since at least I can provide empirical examples of this being the case?

The way people have dealt with this issue varies immensely. Bourdieu himself sees dispositionality as an active force in the sense of "a material causal tendency," as theorized in the tradition of critical realism mentioned earlier. This is the idea that a dispositional force is a causal force. It causes something to happen even when it does not cause the agent to do what it is disposing it to do.[22] So, as in the earlier situation, the police officer is ticketing me and I have a disposition to lose my temper. But even if I don't lose my temper, simply having this disposition might explain why I broke the car's internal door handle that I was furiously clutching while enduring the experience of being ticketed. *Everything in my body* really wanted me to lose my temper and bang him on the head. This *really wanting* is the dispositional force generated by my habitus. It is an active force even though—because of the power of circumstances and the fear of aggravating things—I managed not to lose my temper. Though it did not manifest itself in the form of a loss of temper, it did manifest itself in me breaking the door handle. It could and might have manifested itself in other ways, such as a change in the timbre of my voice as I was being overly polite to the police officer. Thus, a disposition does not have to exteriorize itself as a manifest and distinct happening; it can merely "color" and "shape" what is happening. Either directly or symptomatically it always causes something to happen.

This potential for multivarious expression is crucial for understanding the often hybrid manifestations of habitus. An accent is the clearest example of such a hybridization of what a body is disposed to do and what it finds itself having to do. Let's say I am a native French speaker and therefore have a disposition to speak French. I am learning English, and the teacher asks me to say the word *table*. I look at it and I say *teh'beuhl*. One can see that it is not the French pronunciation of table as *tahbl* that is haunting me; rather it is the task of producing the phonemes *tay* and *ble*. An accent is not a cognitive lack but a state of the body; this means that a disposition is not just a psychological disposition but an inclination of the body. Thus, an accent is produced by uttering sounds against the dispositionality of one's facial, mouth and tongue muscles, and vocal cords. The fact that I eventually might succeed in saying *table* without a French accent means that I have the physiological capacity to do so but that it takes time to acquire the dispositionality. This is why, often enough, the relation between capacity and dispositionality translates into a relation between the biological and the social. One cannot internalize and develop a social disposition of something one has no biological capacity for. Indeed, one might say that the most dominant trope for habitus is perhaps less, as Héran says, the externalization of internalization and more the socialization of asocial generative processes.[23] That is, generative power is an asocial capacity of the body, and the process of internalization is what transforms this asocial capacity into one that is adapted to a social situation and a social milieu. In what follows I want to use an autoethnographic narrative to exemplify and further expand on the question of capacities and dispositions.

Hearing Capacities and Eavesdropping Dispositions

Since I had a cochlear implant in October 2004, I have been writing what I have titled, somewhat inexactly, "an autoethnography of my deafness." Inexactly, because what I am recording includes reminiscences of when I actually started losing my hearing, as well as experiential accounts of hearing with a cochlear implant. In 2010, I was working on some of these notes while concurrently offering my usual seminar on Pierre Bourdieu's work, and I quickly began to note how permeated my autoethnographic language was by the very Bourdieusian concepts I was teaching.

It is, of course, hardly surprising for someone who has been as deeply influenced by Pierre Bourdieu's work as I have to be deploying Bourdieusian categories while writing daily diary-like notes. Nonetheless, not everything lends itself to the deployment of Bourdieusian categories with the same ease. The fact that this account of my deafness did drove me to investigate the extent to which I could use it in the classroom to further clarify what one can gain from—but also what are the limits of—thinking about certain situations with Bourdieusian categories. In what follows I will use parts of these accounts of my hearing loss in a way that highlights and further develops what we have explored so far regarding the nature of habitus and its enmeshment in a political economy of being.

Between the Capacity to Hear and the
Disposition to Eavesdrop

"It is nerve deafness. I am sorry, but there isn't much I can do for you. A hearing aid will not be of much help." I still remember those words very solemnly pronounced by the ear specialist I went to see sometime in 1978. Until that point, I was very much hoping that there was "something he could do for me." But it brought to an end a long period of speculation that began with me noting a year or so earlier, "No, I am not failing to understand what people were saying because of their Australian accent. There is no doubt about it: I am not hearing very well." Three years or so before that visit, in Beirut, in the middle of the Lebanese Civil War and before I left to continue my university studies in Australia, a bomb exploded very close to me. I could not hear well for a couple of days following the explosion. So, immediately I thought that was the obvious culprit. Later tests did not show conclusively that it was. The nature of my nerve deafness and its "curve" was not consistent with an injury, the doctor informed me. There was a possibility that the bomb accelerated already existing damage. After probing into my past, the doctor decided that it could be due to either a preexisting congenital condition or damage to the nerves incurred from years of being a drummer with a distinct bias toward hard rock music. Suddenly I was confronting the possibility that my deafness was the product of both the highs of Beirut's hedonistic culture and the lows of its barbarism.

After arriving in Australia in mid-1976, and particularly when I started university, I began noticing that I was having difficulties following lectures in big lecture halls. I somehow assumed that this must be the Australian accent of the lecturers. And, for a while, I convinced myself that this indeed was my main problem. Somehow I did not let the fact that I had no problems understanding Australian accents in face-to-face or small group situations perturb my reasoning. Much later it dawned on me that the lecturers I had most difficulty following were serious mumblers. But in any case, the conviction that my lack of comprehension was caused by the Australian accent was a short-lived one, for in the back of my mind, there was another experience that was slowly imposing itself on me and that forced me to confront the fact that I was definitely losing my hearing: I was losing my ability to eavesdrop.

Eavesdropping was not something I occasionally indulged in. It was a vice that I engaged in all the time. It was a permanent *disposition* that was part of my very being and the way I defined my viability. This is what makes it good ground for the exemplification of some of the key dimensions of habitus we have examined so far. As a young boy, my parents used to take me often to what was, for me, excruciatingly boring lunches with their friends and business partners. There were no iPhones or iPods at the time. Even the Walkman had not come into existence. I directed my attention to the tables around me, and started eavesdropping to ease the boredom. Even though the conversations at these surrounding tables were not necessarily more interesting than what was happening at my table, I nonetheless derived a pleasure from listening to what seemed like "stolen" conversations. It was an addictive pleasure. It did not take long before I was eavesdropping everywhere, regardless of whether I was stuck in a boring business lunch with my parents or having lunch at my boarding school. I became an eavesdropper. From a situation where I was eavesdropping because I was not interested in the table I was sitting at, I gradually developed through repetition a desire to eavesdrop regardless of what kind of table I was sitting at. The space of the other tables and my body developed an intimate relation such that I became always geared to direct myself toward this other space, rather than or alongside the space of the table where I was sitting. It is in this sense that eavesdropping became a constant natural mode of deploying myself in the world—a disposition that I found rewarding. It augmented my being. Maybe it did so perversely, but it did so nonetheless. That is why losing my ability to engage in it was a seriously painful loss. Using Benedict de Spinoza's language, my deafness and inability to eavesdrop was a decrease in my "perfection" that generated "sadness."[24]

As we have seen, habitus for Bourdieu is both a manifestation and a measurement of this "perfection." It addresses the question, "How well is a body capable of deploying itself in a particular environment?" And, for Bourdieu, the answer is always, "As well as the body has internalized the environment it is inhabiting."

I have mentioned my *capacity* to hear what was going on at the other table, and my social *disposition* to eavesdrop. We can move to further explore the distinction between the two, which is, as we have seen, at the core of the notion of habitus. The first thing the distinction helps us draw attention to is that becoming part of any social space involves the transformation of physiological capacities into social dispositions. The disposition to speak in Arabic is the result of a physiological capacity to speak that has internalized, and coevolved with, an Arabic-speaking social space. One cannot internalize a space and develop a bodily disposition toward something without first having the capacity to develop such a disposition. I cannot develop a disposition to eavesdrop without a physiological capacity to hear. Likewise, I can continuously expose myself to the flight of a bird, but it is not going to make me fly. One should note, however, that this might create in me a disposition to fantasize about flying.

The complexity of the situation lies in the fact that the transformation of physiological capacities into social dispositions does not mean that the physiological is always a capacity and the social always a disposition. A

Structure, Capacity, and Dispositionality

body's power is not always either a capacity or a disposition across social space and time. Capacity is a "raw" or "presocialized" power that the body brings into a social space before being transformed within that space into a disposition. My physiological capacity to hear was the raw material that was transformed, by virtue of me being born in Lebanon, into a disposition to hear Arabic. But this disposition to hear Arabic became a capacity in relation to my disposition to eavesdrop. I brought with me one day to the dinner table my capacity to hear Arabic and, with time, because of the social and historical circumstances I have already related, my capacity to hear Arabic was transformed into a disposition to eavesdrop on people speaking Arabic. A disposition is therefore a capacity—social, physiological, or even biological—that has been transformed through a process of coevolution with a particular social space.

Note that when I started to lose my hearing I didn't immediately lose my disposition to eavesdrop, even though I was losing my capacity to do so (which really amounted to losing my physiological capacity to hear). The relation between capacity and disposition is not unidirectional in a simple way. Indeed, for a while I was in this frustrating state where I had the disposition to eavesdrop without the capacity to do so. This highlights the issue we examined in chapter 1: the way a disposition is a different kind of bodily power, a different phenomenon, from a capacity. To say that I had, like all hearing people, a capacity to eavesdrop simply means that I had all that was essential or necessary for me to do so. This is not the same as saying that I was disposed to eavesdrop, which clearly means more than having these essential elements. It means that I had the urge to do it, that my body was driven to do it. I think the difference is obvious, but its significance is not.

There is another key point discussed in chapter 1 that can be further stressed here. Take two situations, where (1) I have the capacity to eavesdrop and (2) I have the disposition to eavesdrop. The difference does not entail that in case 2, I will definitely eavesdrop, while in case 1, I will not eavesdrop. For neither having a capacity nor having a disposition determines what I will actually do. I might well be disposed to eavesdrop, but this disposition alone doesn't mean that I will. Indeed, if I am in a transitional state following visits to Eavesdroppers Anonymous, I could even say that I am disposed to eavesdrop but have worked out a way to stop myself from doing so. Conversely, on the same table that night, somebody who doesn't have the disposition to eavesdrop might be eavesdropping on the table next to us, because they really want to know what is happening at that particular table. This is what bothered many ancient and modern philosophers about the notion of disposition. In the case above, why not say that I also clearly have a disposition not to eavesdrop since, as mentioned earlier, at least I can provide empirical examples of it being the case?

Here we come to the importance of seeing dispositionality, as Bourdieu does, as an actual constant empirical force that is always present and that causes something to happen even when it does not cause the subject to do what it is disposing it to do. If I am having dinner in a restaurant and I have a disposition to eavesdrop, simply having this disposition will explain why I have to concentrate harder than others in order to stay tuned to the conversation happening around my table. This is the case even if I don't eavesdrop. I will be more tired by the end of the dinner and my tiredness can only be explained by the fact that I had to fight my disposition to eavesdrop in order not to do it. Unlike *having a capacity*, *having a disposition* is an active variable in a given social situation. It has a specific type of causal power even when it does not cause the body to do what it is disposed to do.

Before moving away from the question of dispositionality, there is something quite important that needs to be emphasized. Sometimes, phenomenologically inclined Bourdieusians equate habitus with dispositionality. This is really reducing Bourdieu's anthropology to philosophy. For it is true that habitus, as understood by phenomenologists like Husserl or Merleau-Ponty, can be understood as a form of dispositionality, but this is not true in the case of Bourdieu. Indeed, if that were the case, Bourdieu would not have added much to the philosophical understanding of habitus and should be seen as simply aiming to apply it in empirical research. That is, however, not the case. For Bourdieu, as I have argued, a habitus is not just a dispositionality but the structure of this dispositionality. While in chapter 1, I highlighted the theoretical realism behind the famous definition of habitus as *a structured structure*, a *structuring structure*, and so on, there is another important dimension of this conception of structure that is worth exploring and that elucidates a different relation between dispositionality and structure.

What does this mean in relation to my eavesdropping? Eavesdropping is a disposition, but it also has a general structure: you are physically positioned within one specific space, the table you are sitting at, yet your attention is also—or mostly—directed to another space, the space of a nearby table. Now, if you visit a museum and while you are looking at a painting your attention drifts to thoughts about how others are relating to surrounding paintings, we can say that you have a similarly structured disposition when it comes to visual experiences. And if you are eating from your plate at a restaurant but you cannot help yourself being totally interested in what's on the plate of the person next to you and how they are eating, yet again we can say that you have a similar structure of experience. It is the shared structure of these dispositions that represents habitus for Bourdieu, not the dispositions themselves. That is why he calls it "transposable structure." Theoretically speaking, the lineage of this conception of structure is in Merleau-Ponty's notion of *généralité du corps*. Merleau-Ponty uses the examples of how writing on a paper and on a blackboard involve distinctively different muscles, and yet the general movement of those muscles ends up producing in each case a similar handwriting.[25] While an actual disposition located in a particular part of the body cannot be transferred to another part of the body, the general nature of it can. In much the same way, a hearing disposition cannot be transposed into the domain of smell, but its structure can. This is habitus for Bourdieu, not the disposition on its own. William James touches on this structural transposability when noting that a transformation of women's "muscular feelings" in Norway thanks to skiing will lead to their more general transformation from "sedentary fireside tabby-cats" to "lithe and audacious creatures":

> Consider, for example, the effects of a well-toned *motor-apparatus*, nervous and muscular, on our general personal self-consciousness, the sense of elasticity and efficiency that results. They tell us that in Norway the life of the women has lately been entirely revolutionized by the new order of muscular feelings with which the use of the ski, or long snow-shoes, as a sport for both sexes, has made the women acquainted. Fifteen years ago the Norwegian women were even more than the women of other lands votaries of the old-fashioned ideal of femininity, "the domestic angel," the "gentle and refining influence" sort of thing. Now these sedentary fireside tabby-cats of Norway have been trained, they say, by the snow-shoes into lithe and audacious creatures, for whom no night is too dark or height too giddy, and who are not only saying good-bye to the traditional feminine pallor and delicacy of constitution, but actually taking the lead in every educational and social reform. I cannot but think that the tennis and tramping and skating habits and the bicycle-craze which are so rapidly extending among our dear sisters and daughters in this country are going also to lead to a sounder and heartier moral tone, which will send its tonic breath through all our American life.[26]

For Bourdieu, therefore, my disposition to eavesdrop is only a social habitus insofar as this structure is reproduced in other spaces. In my case, it is. Indeed, I wonder if this disposition to be in one place while directing my attention to what is around it also structures the way I do my research. Even this work on Bourdieu involves attention to the "philosophical table" next to me while sitting at Pierre Bourdieu's dinner table, as it were.

I want to move now to Bourdieu's conception of the habitus–social reality nexus that he developed in dialogue with Husserl's notion of *Umwelt*. This underlies Bourdieu's notion of politics as a struggle, not between views *of* realities but between realities. Again, some reflections on my eavesdropping and later deafness can help illuminate Bourdieu's conceptualization.

Concerning Socially Constructed Realities

The habit of eavesdropping does not merely involve listening to people you are not supposed to listen to. It also situates the listener in a different "hearing reality." I say a different hearing reality because, just as eavesdropping involves a different way of deploying oneself (one's hearing) in the world, it also involves a different way in which the world makes itself present to us. Generally speaking, there is a correlation between the intensity with which one hears a sound and the shortness of the distance between the listener and the source emitting the sound. The closer the sound, the clearer, sharper, and louder it is heard by a hearing person. For an eavesdropper, this order of things is reversed: one occupies a world in which the sounds closest to us are experienced as faint while those further away are sharper. It is important to stress here that this is not a mere "take" on reality but *a reality* (or, rather, both). Indeed, when I lost my capacity to eavesdrop it wasn't a point of view on, or a representation of, reality that I lost but a whole reality that I had inhabited and that was no longer available to me to inhabit. It is this social space, subjectively produced as a result of one's specific interests, social location, and power—but objectively/practically existing nonetheless—that marks Bourdieu's perspectivism. It is a perspectivism that he has produced by blending Friedrich Nietzsche's perspectivism with Husserl's *Umwelt*. Perspectives for Bourdieu are part and parcel of the social realities they bring about, but neither these perspectives nor those social realities are mere subjective takes on reality. They are realities as such, produced by the historical unfolding of a particular habitus and the environment it is part of and that it has brought into being.

This conception already had an embryonic existence in the Aristotelian notion of *hexis*. But it was taken up by Husserl and further developed in his conception of the *Umwelt*.[27] Bourdieu fully activates this Husserlian notion while politicizing it by integrating Nietzsche's perspectivism and arguing that habitus is always metonymic of a larger social reality that is integral to it. Consequently, insofar as life is a struggle between differently dispositioned people with different habitus, life is also a struggle between different realities. This constructivism is radical in that it is not a relativism.[28] Perhaps we can say that Bourdieu's realities are social constructions in the sense of a chair—as a product of human labor—being more a social construction than a tree. While this analogy does not entirely capture the complexity of what is meant by *social construction*, it nonetheless conveys the key idea in Bourdieu's perspectivist social constructivism: To say that something is socially constructed is not an ontological statement regarding how real it is.

In this sense, the accumulation of being that is generated by the habitus does not only pertain to a technical domain of accumulation of practical efficiency. It also embodies a more existential domain that we can call the accumulation of homeliness. One can say, continuing along the same phenomenological, Heideggerian/Husserlian bent, that habitus is a principle of homing and building—of striving to build a space where one can be at home in the world. It is a struggle that is always never ending.[29]

This means that when we say that a habitus "fits" in its environment, it does not purport that there is some kind of imaginary "total fit." Rather, it means that the habitus is part of an environment where it is capable of generating actions that strive to make us at home. This is what Bourdieu refers to as "strategy." Here strategy is quite dissimilar to what is ordinarily understood by the term: a withdrawn, calculating maneuver. Rather, it is a product of the kind of "dexterity" that Bourdieu was seeking to introduce with the notion of the habitus, an "*ars inveniendi* that is neither conscious nor intentional, and so does not allow for ex nihilo, free creation, but which still does not consign the agent to a reproduction of the conditions of the production of his habitus."[30] Bourdieu writes that the "most effective strategies . . . are those which, being the product of dispositions shaped by the immanent necessity of the field, tend to adjust themselves spontaneously to that necessity, without express intention or calculation."[31] Therefore, when the habitus creates or makes "choices," it does so not in spite of the conditions of its production but because of them. The "feel for the game" that derives from attunement to these conditions does not produce a "well-fitting" agent in the sense of how a piece of a puzzle fits by falling into place. Rather, fitting "enables an infinite number of 'moves' to be made, adapted to the infinite number of possible situations which no rule, however complex, can foresee."[32] As Heidegger famously asserts, we are at home insofar as we feel we can strive to be at home.[33] Likewise, for Bourdieu, the habitus is at home insofar as it can generate strategies; strategies are both an indication that the human agent is not totally at home and the fact that they are.

It is in this sense that I was at home in my eavesdropping hearing world. And its loss was, as I have argued, a loss of a home, not the loss of a subjective perspective on the world. Even more clearly, when I lost my capacity to hear, I lost the world that my hearing both created and allowed me to inhabit. I didn't lose a subjectively conceived auditory "perspective" on the world. From such a point of view, our sensorial reality is always the fusion of a multiplicity of realities produced by the encounter of the world with each of the senses.

This conception of social realities as "real constructions," emanating from an encounter between the multiple potentialities of the body and the multiple potentialities of the surrounding environment is, as it were, perhaps one of the more critical and far-reaching aspects of Bourdieu's work. I see it as prefiguring the "multinaturalist" turn developed in the works of Bruno Latour and Eduardo Viveiros de Castro.[34] But it also takes us to where one encounters the limits of Bourdieu's conception of those realities. I will now move to those aspects of my experience of deafness and hearing that point to some of those limits.

Hearing, Listening, Being, and Social Being

The first experience associated with deafness that I want to highlight here has to do with the loss of the symbolic capacity of speech. Being partially deaf meant that I still heard speech. But as I got deafer, speech slowly became unrecognizable and meaningless. Those differences in phonemes and morphemes set against each other, which Ferdinand de Saussure tells us are the basis of the production of meaning,[35] start to disappear, and every word or sentence becomes a certain duration of sound that lacks clear differentiation and therefore meaning. Later, after I received a cochlear implant, I recovered some of this capacity to capture those differences that made sound meaningful, and in the process some of the symbolic sharpness of the world returned.

But here something interesting happened. After the exhilarating period where I gradually felt I was hearing better again, I started to yearn every now and then to the world of deafness which was not as dominated by symbolic or symbolizable dimensions. The way I associated the symbolic domain, or symbolized life, with the "sharpness" of sound was itself interesting to me. I felt that as a deaf person I had a greater access to what I might call the libidinousness of the world and a certain subliminal jouissance came with this slightly less sharp and symbolic relation to what was around me.

Let it be clear that what I experienced and what I am describing is not an either/or situation (i.e., either symbolic or not) but a case of more or less. Perhaps from a Lacanian perspective I can say that the imaginary dimensions of life became a little bit more important as I lost the capacity to hear because the symbolic/representational dimension became a little bit less pronounced.[36] It is not a world without words, but rather that even words themselves, as they lose this sharp differentiation, start conveying less a symbolic meaning and more an emotional charge; instead of differentiated meanings they produce differentiated intensities, something perhaps more akin to Julia Kristeva's *chora*.[37] How can one think of this perspective on reality as a *sui generis* reality as conceived in the Bourdieusian/Husserlian approach described above? Before attempting to think through the answer to this question, I will describe the second experience I want to relate. It has to do with something I only became aware of after I received my cochlear implant.

Going deaf means that hearing requires an exceptional amount of concentration. As you are scraping the bottom of the barrel for a bit of meaning here and there to reconstitute the totality of what is being said to you, you simply cannot afford to lose or let escape anything that it is possible to capture. As such, hearing not only takes the form of an intense listening but also involves an acute reliance on reading lip movement (even when one is not formally trained in lip-reading). It also requires a far more developed visual alertness to body language and, finally, an intense affective attunement to moods that relies on all the senses. It is an exceptionally tiring practice.

When I received my implant and gradually recovered some of the capacity to hear my surroundings, such as birds, airplanes, the wind, cars in the background, or ocean waves, I slowly regained something I had forgotten about completely: Hearing is not always a purposeful act. One simply hears. It is a way of being constantly deployed in the world, but not in the sense of deployment associated with Bourdieu's habitus, where the body is always deployed directionally to do this or that.[38] Here's a passage from the autoethnographic notes I took during the early period when my cochlear implant was being fitted and fine-tuned for me:

> This morning, following the cochlear adjustment session, I sat in the park facing St Vincent's Hospital. The session involved only mild adjustments but for some reason as I was going down the elevator, I felt a sense of qualitative difference in the sounds I was hearing. . . . I thought the same as I did a few weeks ago: "more human and less computer like." As I settle on the park bench I became emotional again hearing the birds just as I did two weeks ago. I was hearing them even better . . . like I remembered them to be . . . I felt lucky and grateful that I've had the opportunity to hear them again . . . and I sat down enjoying the sun in the park. Then my thought drifted to the paper I was writing and I got immersed thinking about it. Suddenly, as I slowly moved back to thinking about more everyday practical things, something struck me. I never stopped hearing the birds, the traffic, car doors slamming, while I was thinking about my writing. I was hearing them in their distinctness even though I was not aiming to hear them. This was definitely a "regained" experience. Hearing my surroundings as a distinct and recognizable sound rather than a general hum, and, as importantly, hearing it without concentrating all my energy in order to do so.

As I reflected on these two realities/experiences in conjunction with thinking about Bourdieu's theory and its relation to philosophy, there was a disruption of the relatively smooth and complementary way in which the relations among the three operated. In concluding this chapter, I want to suggest that this disruption comes because these experiences denote a happening and a reality that lie outside the dominant modern conception of being that Bourdieu works with. As such, they require an anthropology of radical alterity that demands more than the kind of relation Bourdieu's work has with philosophy.

On the Production and
Distribution of the Meaningful Life

3

~~~~~~

In chapter 2, I concentrated on Pierre Bourdieu's notion of habitus, emphasizing the way it provides the anthropological underpinning of an economy of being, where being is centered on the efficient practical deployment of the self within a specific social environment that is felt to be one's own. I argued that such an economy was centered on the production and distribution of modes and degrees of practical social affinity between social agents and society. We looked at how the mind-body assemblage's capacity to classify, categorize, and act in the social world that defines this social affinity is grounded in historically inherited and acquired practical inclinations and social dispositions. In looking at these inclinations and dispositions from the perspective of habitus, I highlighted their physiological nature. I argued that, in that context, inclination is like the inclination of trees on a beach: the history of the wind forces they have been subjected to historically has sculpted them and inclined them in a particular way. Society works on sculpting the human body and gives it inclinations in much the same way. With the notion of *illusio*, Bourdieu invites us to deepen our understanding of the nature of the social agents' *inclinations* and *dispositions*. He invites us to see them not merely as practical but also libidinal and existential. Another figurative way of putting this is to say that habitus defines the inclination we acquire from the social forces that are behind us. *Illusio* defines the inclination we acquire when extending ourselves toward the attachments that are ahead of us and coming our way.

Often, when as a favor we ask someone to perform a task for us, we do not just ask them if they are able to do it; we ask them, "Are you willing and able?" One can think of the difference between habitus and *illusio* in the same way: if habitus is of the order of ability, *illusio* aims to capture the order of willingness. It points not only to whether we can do something, but to how much *it means to us* to do it. The richness of *illusio* as an analytical category is closely related to the richness of the concept of "meaningfulness" present in this formulation. When we say that something means something to us, the notion of "meaning" in English takes us in two main directions. In the first, to say that something means something is to say that it makes sense to us—that the world around us has meaning to us means that we understand it. That is, it is part of our symbolic order: It signifies, denotes, and connotes. It suggests, insinuates, represents, and so on. Here, then, the meaningfulness of the world is of the order of intelligibility. It stands in opposition to the world as incomprehensible and indecipherable. In the second direction, to say that something means something to us is to say that it is important and significant to us, as when we say, "You don't know how much this means to me." We are intimating ideas of value, worth, seriousness, relevance, and consequentiality. Here the meaningfulness of the world stands in opposition to what leaves us indifferent.

In the French language, by contrast, there is a third signification associated with "meaning" that is most central for Bourdieu. "Meaning" in French is *sens*, which has a cognate English term in *sense*. *Sens* in French, however, means not only "meaning" but also "direction." Something that has *sens*, that makes sense, is not only something that is intelligible but is something that points us in a specific direction.[1] Here, then, the meaningfulness of life is associated with the degree to which it allows social agents to "head in a specific direction," to feel like they are "going somewhere" as opposed to "going nowhere." For Bourdieu, this directionality denotes an order of purposefulness captured by another French term, one that is commonly used in English: *raison d'être*, reason to exist. This latter order, purposefulness, has a certain existential primacy for Bourdieu as far as *illusio* is concerned, at least from a phenomenological perspective. To have a purpose in life is to develop interests, and "to understand the notion of interest, it is necessary to see that it is opposed not only to that of disinterestedness or gratuitousness but also to that of *indifference*."[2] To the extent that life has a purpose for social agents, that it gives them reasons to exist, they invest themselves in it. They become attached to their surrounding environment such that it becomes meaningful in both the sense of "intelligible" and "important."

Illusio, then, locates the social agent along three axes: one where life has differing degrees of intelligibility, another where life has differing degrees of significance and importance, and a third where life fluctuates in degrees of purposefulness. These define the parameters of a political economy of being, in which the viability of life is primarily associated with the production and circulation of, and the struggle for, types and degrees of meaningfulness (see fig. 3.1).

On the Production and Distribution of the Meaningful Life

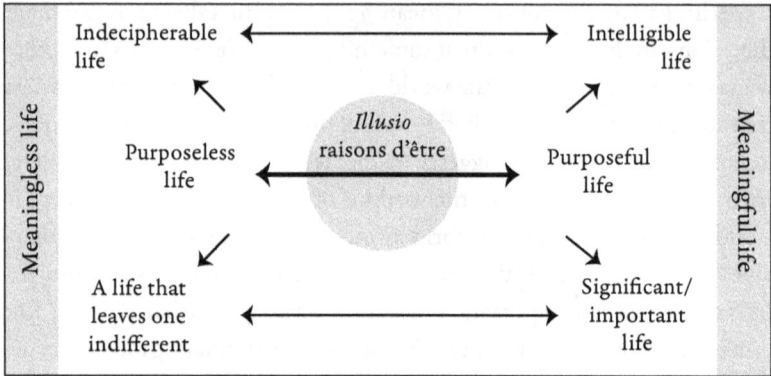

Meaningless life

Indecipherable life ←————————→ Intelligible life

Purposeless life

Illusio raisons d'être

Purposeful life

A life that leaves one indifferent ←————————→ Significant/ important life

Meaningful life

3.1 The three horizontal axes along which *illusio* locates the social agent.

Illusio and the Meaningful Life

Bourdieu takes the concept of *illusio* directly from a famous 1938 book, *Homo Ludens*, by the Dutch historian and cultural theorist Johan Huizinga. The book deals with the social history and social function of play, stressing its centrality in the formation of human culture. On the basis of what is in fact a false etymological relation with *ludere* (play), Huizinga uses *illusio* (or *inlusio*) to define the way people put all of their selves in and become fully absorbed or "taken by the game" when they take a game seriously.[3] Bourdieu's key interest in the concept is in the way Huizinga uses it to undertake a paradoxical juxtaposition of *play* or *game*—which denote frivolity, lack of importance, and the like—with the notion of seriousness.[4] *Illusio* clearly alludes to the notion of "illusion." The illusion referred to here is the illusion of significance and importance acquired by what is at stake in a game the moment players put all of themselves into the game and are taken by it. But, as Bourdieu has often explained, *illusio* is also etymologically linked to *lusiones*, a term used in the seventeenth century to denote chance.[5] This points to the way people, when playing a game seriously, put all of their selves on the line, as it were. They take chances and live at the mercy of the odds of winning or losing in the hope of winning whatever the game has to offer.

Bourdieu transforms Huizinga's conception of the centrality of play in human culture to argue a more existentialist thesis: the idea that life itself, as far as humans are concerned, is best understood as a game—that it is something that lacks any seriousness and significance prior to it being played. Life can only come to exist as a serious endeavor, indeed can come to exist at all, insofar as it is taken seriously: "Taking part in the *illusio* . . . means taking seriously (sometimes to the point of making them questions of life and death) stakes which, arising from the logic of the game itself, establish its 'seriousness.'"[6] According to Bourdieu, then, life "by itself," the unplayed life, as it were, is not necessarily purposeful. It yields a purpose only from the moment we play it seriously. In turn, the lifeworld around us is transformed from an unintelligible mass to a meaningful environment in the very process of life being played seriously. It is in this sense that Bourdieu speaks of "entering life as entering the illusion of the real," or what he calls the "vital illusion."[7] As with Huizinga's players, the degree of significance and importance that life acquires the moment it is lived also has an illusory dimension. It appears to those playing the game of life as if the importance and significance of its stakes are inherent to life itself, but an observer who is not caught in life's games can see that this importance and significance emanate from the way and the degree to which social agents put all of themselves into living it.

At first glance, Bourdieu appears here to be accepting the existentialist thesis that life *in itself* has no intrinsic meaning, no deep significance: the idea that unlike the way it is presented in religious discourse, we do not exist on earth *for* this or that purpose—that is, for any established a priori specific purpose that gives meaning to the world around us.[8] And, to be sure, in the statements above there are clearly definite elements of an ongoing dialogue with existentialism. As Bourdieu explicitly puts it,

> one can establish a necessary link between three indisputable and in-separable anthropological facts: man is and knows he is mortal, the thought that he is going to die is unbearable or impossible for him, and condemned to death, an end (in the sense of *termination*) which cannot be taken as an end (in the sense of *goal*), since it represents, as [Martin] Heidegger put it, "the possibility of the impossibility," he is a being without a reason for being, haunted by the need for justification, legitimation, recognition. And, as Pascal suggests, in this quest for justifications for existing, what he calls "the world," or "society," is the only recourse other than God.[9]

But in this dialogue with existentialism Bourdieu makes what we should by now recognize as a classical critical move against philosophy by arguing that the proper grounds for reflecting on such difficult philosophical questions are social scientific rather than philosophical. The point is not to engage in some abstract reflection about how to snatch meaning from the jaws of cosmic insignificance but to recognize that, despite what appears to the observer as life's intrinsic meaninglessness, people do find the justification to go on living as if life is meaningful. In fact, the experience of the world as "meaningless" can itself be the product of a very scholastic disposition toward the world: "One has to suspend the commitment to the game that is implied in the feel for the game in order to reduce the world, and the actions performed in it, to absurdity, and to bring up questions about the meaning of the world and existence which people never ask when they are caught up in the game."[10]

For those who experience life from the inside, the meaningfulness of life arrives in the very fact of being inserted in society. Hence, the task is social scientific rather than philosophical. It involves showing the many ways in which society itself works as a mechanism for the production and distribution of such meaningfulness. This argument was already present in Bourdieu's inaugural lecture as a professor at the Collège de France: "Pascal spoke of the 'misery of man without God.' One might rather posit the 'misery of man without mission or social consecration.' Indeed, without going as far as to say, with [Émile] Durkheim, 'Society is God,' I would say: God is never anything other than society. What is expected of God is only ever obtained from society, which alone has the power to justify you, to liberate you from facticity, contingency and absurdity."[11] It remains a key argument in Bourdieu's later work: "The social world gives what is rarest, recognition, consideration, in other words, quite simply reasons for being. It is capable of giving meaning to life, and to death itself, by consecrating it as the supreme sacrifice."[12]

Bourdieu, then, invites us to see the social world as an economy geared toward the social production and distribution of *raisons d'être,* offering the social agents that inhabit it varieties of paths and avenues for self-realization. Going on such paths can be more or less all-encompassing, more or less satisfying, and more or less desirable, but it is nonetheless an experience of *the possibility of a life worth living* and worth struggling to achieve. As they go along such a path, social agents begin the process through which they capture and are captured by an *illusio*: an experience of the meaningfulness of their world and the meaningfulness of their own selves as intrinsic to life itself rather than as something socially produced.

That *illusio* is as much about the production of a meaningful world around us as it is about the production of meaningful selves should be clear. The two processes go hand in hand. In distributing *raisons d'être,* society is distributing both social realities that are experienced as worthwhile and senses of personal significance. As Bourdieu notes, "'Entering into life,' as one says, means to accept entering into one or another of the social games which are socially recognized, and engaging in the inaugural investment, both economic and psychological, which is implied in the participation in the serious games of which the social world is composed. This belief in the game, in the value of a game, and of its stakes, is manifested above all . . . in seriousness, indeed in the very spirit of seriousness, this propensity to take seriously all things and people—especially oneself."[13]

If the viability of the self captured by habitus is closely linked to the ability of the mind-body assemblage to deploy itself efficiently in the world and establish a practical relation of intimacy with it, the "viability of the self" captured by *illusio* is linked to the degree to which social agents take their lives seriously and have a vested interest in living it.

Investing the Self

The idea of "taking oneself seriously" is at the core of Huizinga's conceptualization of *illusio.* As he sees it, there is a relation between taking oneself seriously and taking the game seriously to the point of "putting all of oneself into the game." It is this idea that Bourdieu reconceptualizes as the process of "investing the self" in social reality. It is here that the etymological relation between *illusio* and *lusiones* comes to the fore. It conjures ideas of *chance, probability* of a *return,* or a *yield* on one's investments. All these terms are appropriate, since the concept is designed to allude to the probability of gains (of augmenting one's being) that come as a result of throwing oneself into, investing in, or gambling with oneself in the game of life. But, unlike the entry into Huizinga's games, in Bourdieu's game there is an existential compulsion behind the need to take the world seriously enough to have interests, invest oneself in it, and become preoccupied by it: social agents are "exposed and endangered in the world, faced with the risk of emotion, lesion, suffering, sometimes death, and therefore obliged to take the world seriously."[14]

The idea of gambling with oneself intimates better than other ideas that there is no guarantee of a satisfying yield when one is "investing oneself" in the world. One can then wonder how, on such shaky and uncertain grounds, investment in the social world "offers humans that which they most totally lack: a justification for existing."[15] The answer for Bourdieu might appear paradoxical at first sight: The justification for existing can only be so *because* of the lack of guarantee rather than despite it. This is because the lack of guarantee makes every investment of the self a *pursuit*. And it is through the pursuit itself and the expectation of profits, not through their realization, that this "justification for existing" arises.

Bourdieu is here on well-trodden, yet important, existential territory. In his famous meditation on the relation between building and being, "Building Dwelling Thinking," Heidegger famously begins by stating the commonsense conception of the relation between building and dwelling: "We attain to dwelling, so it seems, only by means of building." But then, through a reflection on the etymological roots of the word *Bauen* (building), he argues that "the proper meaning of the verb *bauen*, namely, to dwell, has been lost to us." He establishes a common root among building, dwelling, and being. This leads him to reach the conclusion that "the way in which you are and I am, the manner in which we humans *are* on the earth, is *Buan*, dwelling. To be a human being means to be on earth as a mortal. It means to dwell." From this, Heidegger deduces a reversal of the commonsense understanding of the relation between building and dwelling that he had started with, the idea that "we build in order to dwell." Instead, Heidegger argues, we build because this is how we dwell, how we *be*: "We do not dwell because we have built, but we build and have built because we dwell, that is because we are *dwellers*."[16] We do not build homes and then dwell/be in them. We dwell / are in the very process of building homes. To smuggle in our own Bourdieusian/Spinozan language, we can say that it is in the process of building a house, and not at the moment we finish it and possess it, that we augment our being. Bourdieu quotes Pascal approvingly as having established this Heideggerian common sense long before Heidegger did: "Through the social games it offers, the social world provides something more and other than the apparent stakes: the chase, Pascal reminds us, counts as much as, if not more than, the quarry, and there is a happiness in activity which exceeds the visible profits—wage, prize or reward—and which consists in the fact of emerging from indifference (or depression), being occupied, projected towards goals, and feeling oneself objectively, and therefore subjectively, endowed with a social mission."[17]

Indeed, as Bourdieu points out, Pascal could see that to highlight the chase is not merely to say that one is invested in process rather than in

68

Chapter 3

outcome. It is to highlight that the process (the chase, the building, the running after our goals) has a specific existential quality that the goal itself never has. Pascal writes, "[Those philosophers] who believe that people are quite unreasonable to spend a day hunting a hare that they would not even have wanted to buy, scarcely know our nature. The hare would not save us from the sight of death . . . but the hunt does."[18]

The process of investing ourselves in reality establishes a space through which we, as beings driven in pursuit of our investments' yield, construct the viability of our social being. In seeing in *illusio* the source of a "driven-ness," a kind of motor that drives our being into the world, Bourdieu consciously introduces an energetic/vitalistic and an affective dimension into the concept. Indeed, as mentioned earlier, he often speaks of the *illusio* as the *vital illusion*. For him to see in *illusio* an actual life force animating the body aligns the notion with a whole "energetics" that runs through all his dispositional concepts. As Stéphane Chevallier and Christiane Chauviré point out, "There is a specific intentionality, a practical one, embedded in the concept of disposition which arises from it being bodily fixed in a specific mode of existence, in the power-to-be (*pouvoir-être*) of the socialized body. This power-to-be does not represent a sleeping force but a real vital momentum insofar as it constitutes the particular expression of a fundamental energy directed at investing oneself in the world and which is always present in the living body."[19]

To have an *illusio* is to become "socially animated." It is to feel social life pumping into one such that one feels propelled into the world. It is not surprising, therefore, that by putting our social being on the line our investments become "questions of life and death."[20] Being a gamble, where we are putting our social life on the line, every investment we are contemplating brings the possibility of our social death, and as such pursuing and struggling for a successful yield becomes itself a struggle against social death in which the whole body-mind assemblage is participating.

With such a conception of investment it is hardly surprising that the concept of libido makes a markedly increased appearance in the work of Bourdieu, sometimes used interchangeably with *illusio*, until it becomes a serious member of his conceptual community in *Pascalian Meditations*, with a whole section devoted to the relation between libido and *illusio*.[21] This simply extends an argument that is already present in his earlier work: "The term 'investment' . . . must be understood in the dual sense of economic investment—which it objectively always is, though misrecognized—and the sense of affective investment which it has in psychoanalysis."[22]

On the Production and Distribution of the Meaningful Life

It is certain that Bourdieu's usage of the notion of libido meets a wish to situate desire at the limit of the biological and the social, in the same way Sigmund Freud situates the drive at the limit of the somatic and the psychic.[23] Bourdieu, however, unlike Freud, does not distinguish libido and drive in his usage of the term *libido*, so as not to reinvite a new dualistic conception of the bodily and the psychic. As such, libido for Bourdieu is, as it is for Gilles Deleuze and Carl Jung, general and desexualized; it appears like a fundamental but nonspecific energy.[24] Yet, unlike in Deleuze's work, it is not a necessary principle of free creativity but something that is channeled in all kinds of ways by institutions, in such a manner approximating Freud's conception. Libido becomes to *illusio* what biological tendencies of the body are to habitus. *Illusio* is socialized libido. We can see how closely Bourdieu flirts with psychoanalysis here and, indeed, in *Pascalian Meditations* he is openly inviting some kind of complementary research program: "The initial form of *illusio* is investment in the domestic space, the site of a complex process of socialization of the sexual and sexualization of the social. And sociology and psychoanalysis should combine their efforts (but this would require them to overcome their suspicion) to analyze the genesis of investment in a field of social relations, thus constituted as an object of interest and preoccupation, in which the child is increasingly implicated and which constitutes the paradigm and also the principle of investment in the social game."[25]

This affective/psychoanalytic dimension is important to help highlight the specificity of Bourdieu's political economy of being. This is so despite its reliance on such terms as *investment, yield, profit,* and *interest,* which can have—and indeed do have—much in common with capitalist economic behavior and terminology as we know them. As with all investments, people can act more conservatively or adventurously. Some investments are safer than others. Some can, with the promise of a higher yield, take the social agent outside what is considered safe, and some are predictable and reproduce a given order, such as when inheritors are "inherited by their inheritance"[26]—that is, when they identify as heirs and pursue lives they have been predisposed to succeed in pursuing due to their inheritance and the reality into which they have been born. There are, however, also important differences between them that the affective or psychoanalytic dimension points to. For, after all, this is an economy of being in which the main aim of an investment is to produce degrees and types of viability of the self that are associated with the degrees and types of reasons to exist that one yields in the process of investing. For instance, *illusio* points to the way viability takes the form of self-valorization: a primary narcissism associated with the *raison d'être*.[27] This is because the latter is closely linked to a "belief in oneself." Such a belief is indeed an important currency of the economy of being that concerns us here—that is, the augmentation of being in this economy is closely associated with an augmentation of belief in one's own value. One can note immediately how such an economy of being, with its psychosocial affective undertones, differs from our common idea of an economy. For instance, as with Benedict de Spinoza's affective economies, augmentation does not necessarily mean "accumulation," since one can accumulate too much belief in oneself: arrogance, haughtiness, self-deceit, and self-importance. Such overaccumulation is often paradoxically the result of social locations that do not yield enough "belief in oneself" and predispose the social agents that occupy them to strategies of overcompensation. Regardless, all such forms of overaccumulation of "belief in oneself" end up translating into a decline rather than in an augmentation of being.

Illusio as an Analytic Category

As the outline above shows, Bourdieu appears, on the one hand, to agree with the existentialist philosophers of his time that, when reflected on philosophically, life appears devoid of intrinsic meaning. But, on the other hand, he sees this view as specific to those who gaze at the world from the outside, scholastically. As such, while agreeing that there is an illusion, he refuses to see the meaningfulness that people derive from the social world as mere delusion. One way to begin unraveling this paradox is to highlight that, at the core of *illusio* is not so much an illusion about the meaningfulness of reality as much as an illusion about where one experiences the meaningfulness as emanating from. People experience life as if it had an intrinsic meaningfulness, while in fact the meaningfulness is socially produced. Those who are caught up in the game of social life, who accept the stakes and meaning of the game, have a perspective on the game that excludes questioning the game itself. The questioning is for the questioners of life, the philosophers and the social scientists, not for those living it, even if people obviously can be both. As Bourdieu states, "The game presents itself to someone caught up in it, absorbed in it, as a transcendent universe, imposing its own ends and norms unconditionally . . . *illusio* is an illusion or 'diversion' only for someone who perceived the game from the outside, from the scholastic standpoint of an 'impartial spectator.'"[28]

The illusion of the *illusio*, here, is thus a naturalization and an enchant-ment of a social process. This makes revealing the social process behind the illusion disenchanting. This has more than a passing similarity to the enchantment of the commodity form in what Karl Marx calls commodity fetishism, for both call for careful attention in understanding the notion of illusion. Most important, one has to avoid giving it an epistemological and mentalistic twist.

In a commonsense way, we are predisposed to interpret the "illusion" that comes with *illusio* along such lines as "*illusio* means that people have the illusion that life is meaningful in itself (i.e., they misperceive and fan-tasize about what reality is), when in fact—in reality—that is not so." This differentiation between what people think or perceive life to be like and what life actually is, or what it is "in fact," implies that some people see life "correctly" and some see it "incorrectly." It also makes it out as if behind the illusion of the *illusio* is a cognitive/epistemological problem concern-ing the incorrect way people perceive and think about reality. This is far from where Bourdieu wants to take us. For him the illusion that comes with the *illusio* is practical and experiential, not merely cognitive. *Illusio*, he tells us, is "produced by the experience of the game."[29] Even when he argues that *illusio* is a matter of "belief" in the game, it is important to re-member that for him "belief" is not merely a cognitive matter but "a state of the body," as he famously put it in *The Logic of Practice*.[30]

This takes us to Bourdieu's ontological perspectivism, as discussed in previous chapters: Reality is one's relation to reality, and it comes forth as a result of the mind-body assemblage's mode of insertion in and interac-tion with its surrounding environment. Thus, to say that *illusio* is of the order of the illusory is to say that any illusory dimension belongs to reality itself, as it is experienced and produced from a particular perspective, and not to our mistaken understanding of it. This is where the question of illusion links *illusio* to Marx's ontological theory of ideology, found in his analysis of commodity fetishism.[31] Marx argues that it is not the people interacting with commodities who have inverted representations of the world of commodities; it is the world of commodities that offers itself to them in an inverted form. It is the very reality of capitalism itself as it is experienced by the consumer that is upside down. There is nothing wrong with people's cognitive capacities; the problem is with reality, as it were.

The best way to exemplify the above is to think about our experience of the movement of the sun: We all experience and speak of the sun ris-ing and the sun going down. We do so even though we have all learned at school that an "astronomical/scientific gaze" tells us that it is the earth that is turning around the sun. That is, knowing and accepting "the truth about the sun" offered by science does not stop us from experiencing our world as if it is the sun that is moving, or from speaking about it in this way. The right knowledge does not "straighten up" our experience. This is because the experience is not the product of faulty knowledge but of the very way the sun presents itself to us in practice. This was nicely put by Maurice Godelier long ago when he wrote, "It is not the subject who deceives himself, but reality which deceives him."[32]

With his theory of commodity fetishism, Marx proceeds not only with an analysis of the upside-down nature of the world of commodities but with an analysis of how this inverted reality comes into being. He engages in a multiperspectival analysis of capitalism. Marx offers us the perspective of capitalist consumers as they interact with commodities, and his own analytical perspective on their perspective allows us to understand how commodities come to be experienced as having a life of their own. In much the same way, with *illusio*, Bourdieu provides us—as he did with the category *habitus*—with an analytical concept that aims to capture the world both phenomenologically and analytically. It offers us both a way of closely experiencing the meaningfulness of life as it is experienced by people in their everyday life and a way of being distant from it so as to analyze how this meaningfulness arises, as if naturally—that is, how it comes to be experienced as intrinsic to life itself rather than something socially produced.

For Bourdieu, the key point of understanding this process of naturalization comes from an understanding of the slow and seemingly unconscious way in which people come to invest themselves into the realities that surround them. As Bourdieu puts it, "the transaction is extremely long . . . one no longer knows who does the choosing, whether it's the institution that chooses the individual or the inverse."[33] As with habitus, this process of naturalization is an essentially sociohistorical one. That is, developing an interest in reality and investing oneself in it are not acts that happen in one instance, as a single event in time, but an ongoing process. This is what makes "being interested and invested in reality" a mode of being. Bourdieu is always keen to remind his listeners and readers of the etymological roots of interest—*inter-esse* means *being in, participating*.[34] That is, the concept invites us to see that being invested in social reality, and being tout court, is an ongoing reciprocal relation with reality. To understand this reciprocal relation of investment we need to examine the slow way through which a particular social milieu evolves historically—in particular, the way it does

On the Production and Distribution of the Meaningful Life

so by giving birth both to social agents with inheritances and orientations toward life and to certain compatible routes of self-realization: As Bourdieu notes, "By investment I mean the propensity to act that is born of the relation between a field and a system of dispositions adjusted to the game it proposes, a sense of the game and of its stakes that implies at once an *inclination* and an *ability* to play the game, both of which are socially and historically constituted rather than universally given."[35]

It is through being born at the same time and in relation to each other that the affinity between the agents' orientations toward certain paths in life and the available paths comes into being. The merging of the two is experienced as quasi-natural and as requiring little social effort. As Bourdieu puts it, "the habitus and the field maintain a relationship of mutual attraction, and the illusion [*illusio*] is determined from the inside, from impulses that rush toward a self-investment in the object."[36] This slow historical process of affective rapprochement is at the same time an elective choice that appears inevitable and an inevitable choice that appears elective: "The original investment has no origin, because it always precedes itself and, when we deliberately enter into the game, the die is already more or less cast."[37]

There is no immaculate choice, then, that one makes to accept the *illusio* prevailing in a given milieu; rather, "one is born into the game, with the game."[38] Bourdieu adds that the "relation of investment, *illusio*, is made more total and unconditional by the fact that it is unaware of what it is." The *illusio* becomes embedded in the body—in the form of an interest in what happens, a corporeal belief unresponsive to conscious interrogation—from a young age, such that the "earlier a player enters the game and the less he is aware of the associated learning . . . the greater is his ignorance of all that is tacitly granted through his investment in the field and his interest in its very existence and perpetuation and in everything that is played for in it."[39]

Illusio highlights that for Bourdieu every anthropology of experience is in some way an anthropology of religion. This is implicit in statements like, "In the beginning is the *illusio*."[40] It becomes almost explicit when he says that *illusio* is the "fact of being caught up in the game, of believing the game is 'worth the candle.'"[41] The idea that the game is "worth the candle" alludes to the Christian practice of lighting a candle for a saint. One lights candles for the saints that one truly believes in—that is, when one believes in their reality and the reality of their powers. It is in this sense that any belief in the real has a religious dimension and its analysis involves an anthropology of religion. The questions associated with such an anthropology are usually of the order of, How can one analyze religious belief without being a believer, and how can one analyze belief if one is a believer?[42] For Bourdieu these questions are true of every experience from which subjects derive a sense of meaningfulness emanating from a "belief in reality." How can one capture the reality of a people's experience of meaningfulness and remain outside those experiences? Bourdieu's whole methodology concerns the possibility of taking a group's *illusio* seriously and yet being able to step back to capture it as *illusio*. As we have seen, Bourdieu negotiates this difficulty—and it is a difficulty that can only be negotiated, rather than "solved"—by stressing the importance of a multiplicity of perspectives that involve taking as one's analytic object the way people themselves construct their viability within their own practices while at the same time remaining reflexively conscious of one's gaze as an analytical one, a gaze that has its own specificity and that introduces into the object its very relation to the object.

75

Elements of a Political Economy of the Meaningfulness of Life

In his prologue to *The Rules of Art* (1995), "Flaubert, Analyst of Flaubert," Bourdieu describes the protagonist, Frédéric, in Gustave Flaubert's *L'éducation sentimentale* as characterized by a "powerlessness to take the real—that is, the stakes of games called serious—seriously."[43] Frédéric's incapacity to take the social world seriously leads him to *play* at social roles as an actor would—as Jean-Paul Sartre's waiter in *Being and Nothingness* ostensibly does[44]—instead of becoming what he is socially marked to be. He "lacks what the bourgeois calls a serious side," which leads him to invest himself insufficiently in life, dispersing his energies among various incommensurable pursuits.[45] In doing so, Frédéric rejects the implicit position already sketched out for him, seeing the "games" of the social world *as games*, while the other characters—especially those who "win" in Flaubert's novel—believe in the intrinsic value and seriousness of the games they play, and therefore misrecognize them, seeing them as everything but arbitrary. Their belief in their respective games is manifested above all "in seriousness, indeed in the very spirit of seriousness, this propensity to take seriously all things and people—especially oneself—socially designated as serious, and them alone."[46]

Frédéric, disposed to approach the world in a particular way because of his inheritance and trajectory, floats above the social world, "*without gravity* (another word for seriousness),"[47] failing to be occupied or taken up by it.

Instead, he rejects as arbitrary the social games that others seriously invest themselves in. He rejects the "*illusio* as an illusion unanimously approved and shared, hence as an illusion of reality."[48] His very being therefore serves to illustrate two facts: first, that the "entry into life as entry into the illusion of the real guaranteed by the whole group is not self-evident,"[49] that one is not necessarily destined to misrecognize the arbitrary as necessary (thereby further illustrating that what is taken as necessary is in fact arbitrary), and second, that the *illusio* cannot be reduced to mere "illusion," as its presence has real effects. Without the collectively agreed-on stakes of a "game," there would be nothing to "play" for and therefore no "players." Far from being an arbitrary construct that one condescendingly distances oneself from, the *illusio* is the necessary arbitrary that holds together all social endeavors.

While Frédéric is a fictional character, Bourdieu takes him seriously because he takes Flaubert seriously as a sociologist. He sees in *L'éducation sentimentale* a kind of imaginary experimental space that is as close as can be to a fantasized social science laboratory—something impossible to obtain in the real world.[50] The experiment highlights the fact that people are not always predestined merely to follow along the path they have inherited. Some born in the midst of a social transformation inherit, but they find their inheritance unsuited to the social world they have inherited.[51] The extent to which people embark on a meaningful path that satisfies them and augments their being is always a "more or less" question. Nor is it the case that people must passively accept the direction in which their investment seems to be heading. People are continually working on valorizing the path along which they find themselves or willfully changing that path if necessary. The world is full of people whose investment of themselves in a social path ends up not yielding what it promised to yield. That is indeed why that investment is an *illusio*, something of the order of a gambling with oneself.

Regardless, what is important is that when moving from theoretical generalizations to dealing with specific individual or collective cases, it is quite obvious that people's ability to embark on a satisfying path in life varies enormously and is never an either/or question. Bourdieu's own empirical case studies are teeming with such cases where social power relations are reflected in an unequal distribution in meaningful lives and an unequal distribution of the capacity to embark on a meaningful life.[52] Sometimes this has to do with some impoverished social milieus that are unable to offer much, and at other times it is because of an impoverished social agent who is not able to embark on what life has to offer. This is the very reason why we speak of a political economy of being.

There are a number of key components of such a politics in Bourdieu's work. The first has to do with the relation between *illusio* and *collusio*. The latter, as the word clearly implies, has to do with the degree to which a collective sanctifies and legitimizes particular individual pursuits. This is not always a case of conformity. As Bourdieu clearly shows in his analysis of the artistic avant-garde, some *collusios* thrive on a valorization of the unique and the nonconventional.[53]

Another important dimension has to do with what Bourdieu calls "social aging." The latter can accompany physiological aging, but does not necessarily do so. It relates to the gradual ossification that comes with sustained investment in *particular* pursuits in life and the shrinking of the ability to diversify into other paths in life. Investing in activities has the effect of "restricting the range of initially acceptable possibilities" so that what once lay before the agent as a myriad of potential undertakings diminishes.[54] What defines *youth* from this perspective is that someone has been following a particular path for only a short time and therefore their mind-body assemblage has not been as marked by as enduring social, affective, and physiological inclinations as would be the case for someone who has spent a lifetime along such a path.[55] It remains more malleable and open to embark on different investments. It is the difference between asking a lifelong professional tennis player to switch to playing squash, or a lifelong French speaker to switch to English. It is therefore a mark of the political economy of meaningfulness that people are less and less able to embark on new paths. Bourdieu describes the process with the analogy to the bifurcations of a tree: "Social aging certainly is measured by the number of changes in position within the social structure, and these changes result in restricting the range of initially acceptable possibilities; or, in other words, it is measured by the bifurcations of the tree which, with its innumerable dead branches, represents a career or retrospectively, a curriculum vitae."[56]

He suggests that as one's investment of time accrues and the virtual "lateral possibles" gradually dissolve,[57] a psychological mechanism is triggered, enabling the agent to see the life with which he has been left as "elected" rather than etched out for him in advance. This "amor fati" gets "agents to act as accomplices in their own destiny,"[58] so that the social aging process requires the "the slow renunciation or disinvestment (socially assisted and encouraged) which leads agents to adjust their aspirations to their objective chances, to espouse their condition, become what they are and to make do with what they have."[59]

For a Creative Usage of Bourdieu's Concepts

Of all of Bourdieu's concepts, *illusio* has been by far the most productive in my own research. I have deployed it analyzing white supremacists' identification in Australia, arguing that what marks supremacist forms of identification is that whiteness in itself becomes an *illusio*: something whose pursuit gives the supremacists' lives a meaning. In a totally different way, in my research on migration I found it useful to show how migration itself becomes a meta-*illusio*.[60] That is, for the would-be immigrant, migration itself is not a particular, satisfying pursuit, such as a professional path; nonetheless, an investment in migration becomes an investment in a path that opens up the possibility of particular life pursuits. Often it is that general path toward more particular paths that is blocked in the home country. Another research domain where I usefully activated the concept of *illusio*, and again, in a completely different way, is in my research with Christian Lebanese militiamen who were unsuccessful in reintegrating into Lebanese society after the Lebanese Civil War. Looking at their lives through the concept of *illusio* allowed me to understand something that was otherwise very difficult to understand. At one point in my research I became interested in how fixated the militiamen were on the unpleasant idea that the war had ended with their defeat. It is not that this interpretation was unrealistic. What was peculiar was the way in which they seemed to desire to dwell within their defeat rather than forget it. It took me a while to understand that, for them, defeat was an *illusio*. It was so because they yielded more being by seeing themselves and being seen by others as defeated fighters than as unemployed and unemployable people in a postwar economy.[61] While as unemployed men they were just "useless bums," defeated fighters were still "fighters," even if defeated.

I am highlighting these examples where I have deployed *illusio* because none of them offers an "orthodox" and a straightforwardly Bourdieusian way of using the concept. If I were to get bogged down by such ideas as, "Oh, maybe I am too voluntaristic in the way I am deploying the concept here," I probably would not have been able to benefit from it. But I did. Not that it necessarily matters, but I also like to report that Bourdieu himself was aware of my unorthodox usage of his concept, at least in the first two instances, and while he had some misgivings and critiques, he wasn't outraged, nor did he try to discourage me from following such a path.

I am saying this because I often hear students and sometimes colleagues who use a certain bogey of Bourdieu as "deterministic" to stop themselves and others from working creatively with his concepts. There is a certain irony in this. As if predestined to be the incarnation of their own deterministic and lifeless understanding of Bourdieu's conceptualization of social subjects, it is often those who seem to inherit an overly rigidly and unimaginatively interpreted Bourdieu, and who are unwilling to take the necessary liberties to transform his work to suit their own research needs, who seem to be the ones most often arguing that his conception of agency creates social agents who assume their inheritances too rigidly and unimaginatively and who are unable to transform their inheritance to suit their own needs.

79

In concluding this chapter, and on a different matter, it is important to remind ourselves that Bourdieu's political economy of being is both an economy of practical affinity that we have associated with habitus and an economy of meaningfulness underpinned *by illusio*. It is both at the same time, not one or the other. Habitus and *illusio* offer us analytical angles on different dimensions of the same economy of being where the two are entangled. Capital, as we shall see in chapter 4, offers another entangled dimension. I am only presenting each separately for heuristic purposes.

Capital is the most diffuse and internally differentiated concept in Pierre Bourdieu's work. It comes in several well-known generic guises—mainly, economic capital, cultural capital, and social capital. These three are often referred to as "resources" and "aces" in a game. Economic capital is the most straightforward; despite a terminological coincidence, it has no relation with the Marxist concept of capital and is merely the equivalent of material wealth.[1] Bourdieu defines it essentially as that which is "immediately and directly convertible into money."[2] Cultural capital is implicit and explicit cultural know-how, the capacity to recognize and manipulate cultural codes.[3] Social capital refers to the durable networks (such as friends and family) and their resources that one can mobilize to achieve one's goals.[4] Bourdieu also tells us that capital can come in different forms: objectified, institutionalized, and incorporated.[5] Cultural capital, in particular, also comes in an infinity of specific forms: academic capital, artistic capital, literary capital, linguistic capital, and so on. In this chapter, capital will be examined from the general perspective elaborated on in this book. Thus, the main question I am asking is this: What kind of conception of human viability does capital point to and what form of political economy of being does it help us elucidate?

The originality of Bourdieu's conceptions of cultural and symbolic capital is difficult to convey decades after he first offered and deployed them, given how much they have been routinized not just in academia but even in the everyday language of educated people. Saying that someone is wealthy but poor in cultural capital circulates well beyond the academy. Ethnographically, capital has offered and continues to offer an angle on social phenomena that is both analytically and methodologically enriching. On the one hand, the usage of capital can be formulaic and banal: If I yearn and struggle to be an academic, I am struggling to accumulate "academic capital," or if I direct my energy at being a bureaucrat, I am also directing my energy toward accumulating "bureaucratic capital." But asking the question "*What* is it that I actually accumulate to accumulate academic or bureaucratic capital?" is ethnographically productive and demanding. Even the formulaic and banal becomes less so when such questions are directed at topics often perceived in the logic of either/or, rather than in the logic of the "more or less" that capital invites one to engage in. Think, for instance, of the implication of saying, "If one desires to be a male (whichever way one defines it) one directs their energy at accumulating 'maleness.'"[6] The idea that people are more or less male—or female or queer—offers a refreshing analytic on the question of identification. In my book *White Nation*, subjecting Australianness to the analytic logic of capital was a particularly critical and productive move. While Australian nationalists often position themselves politically within the nation through either/or questions like "Are you or are you not Australian?," merely to highlight the fact that there are many instances where people frame Australianness in "more or less" terms in itself had a critical political effect on the field of national belonging. To further explore what it is—what kind of capital—that people accumulate to succeed in making claims of being "more Australian" was also ethnographically revealing. This ranged from obvious things, such as birthplace and accent, to less obvious things, such as Christianity and modes of walking.[7]

As we shall later examine in more detail (though it should already be clear here), capital is both what I struggle to accumulate and what I struggle to impose a definition of. If I am positioned in the field of Australian maleness, which means it is taken for granted that Australian maleness matters to me, I am struggling to accumulate Australian maleness in order to be more "Australian male" than others. But I am also struggling to ensure the ascendancy of my version of what Australian maleness involves, that is, the subcapitals I have to accumulate.

As with other Bourdieusian categories, to fully grasp the analytical scope of "capital" one needs to be aware of the variety of critical engagements with different intellectual traditions that it is continually performing. At the time of its genesis, the project of an "economy of symbolic forms," the "original insight that there are immaterial forms of capital . . . as well as material or economic" ones, as Craig Calhoun puts it,[8] presents itself as an interaction with two analytical strands: first, as an engagement with Marxism about the "relative autonomy of the cultural," and second, as an engagement with economism against the modernist view that "only money matters," a view that Bourdieu considers equally "a form of ethnocentrism."[9] In this respect Bourdieu's capital offers a way, already established by Max Weber, of reintegrating the premodern economy of honor into the sociology of capitalist societies.[10] As Bourdieu puts it, "I think I am not one of those who transpose economic concepts uncritically into the area of culture, but I wanted—and not just metaphorically—to establish an economy of symbolic phenomena and to study the specific logic of the production and circulation of cultural goods."[11]

The deployment of capital as an analytic category is an affirmation that there continues to be an economy of prestige that is worth taking into account and studying when analyzing modern societies. This opposes a political economy that accepts the differentiation of fields as a lived reality and treats the production and circulation of material wealth as its only subject matter.[12] As such, it is central for a conceptualization of a political economy of being, whereby being is a total social fact, as it were—something that, like Marcel Mauss's gift, is at the same time economic, political, affective, spiritual, and the like.[13]

For obvious reasons, the category of *capital*, unlike habitus or *illusio*, has the most affinity with economic logic as we know it. It is the most open to a logic of accountancy. Bourdieu speaks of the "volume" of capital, its "conversion rates," "profits," and "investments." As an example of this affinity, observe how Bourdieu portrays gratuitous practices as investments: "Many of the expenditures that are called conspicuous are in no way a squandering and, as well as being obligatory elements in a certain style of life, they are very often—like engagement parties—an excellent investment in social capital."[14]

At the same time, it is not immediately clear in what way capital introduces something new into this political economy of being. From one angle it is hard to differentiate it from the order of practical efficiency analyzed by habitus or the order of raison d'être captured by *illusio*. At best it comes across as the currency of the economy of being delineated by these two concepts: "Tell me how much symbolic capital you have and I'll tell you how much being you've accumulated." As we shall see, it is all this. But it also opens up a dimension of social viability that is specifically its own. Another important dimension of capital's multidimensionality is that it crosses from an anthropological category concerned with the nature of social agents and their pursuit of being to a sociological category concerned with the nature of society. It is crucial for the conceptualization of "fields" that Bourdieu sees, above all, as a relational space constituted by a particular distribution of and a relation between different forms and amounts of capital.

Capital Between Habitus and *Illusio*

As noted above, there is a reading that leaves one wondering in what way capital enriches our conception of a political economy of being. Too often Bourdieu speaks of it as a possession that confers practical "strength" according to how much capital one possesses.[15] This firmly positions capital in an economy of efficacity, and even an economy of efficiency, to recall the distinction made in chapter 1. In a well-known piece, Bourdieu is very explicit: the possession of capital is the possession of efficiency. He highlights the importance of "discovering the powers or *forms of capital* which are or can become efficient, like aces in a game of cards, in this particular universe, that, in the struggle (or competition) for the appropriation of scarce goods of which this universe is the site."[16] In *Invitation to Reflexive Sociology* Bourdieu and Loïc J. D. Wacquant argue that "a species of capital is what is efficacious in a given field, both as a weapon and as a stake of struggle, that which allows its possessors to wield a power, an influence, and thus to *exist*, in the field under consideration, instead of being considered a negligible quantity."[17]

When we are dealing specifically with cultural capital, capital not only belongs clearly to the order of savoir faire and efficiency; equated as it often is with cultural know-how, it becomes hard to know what the difference between capital and habitus is.

We can try to escape this collapsing of the two categories by quickly thinking something like, "I know . . . capital as 'aces' highlights its nature as a 'possession'—a word Bourdieu actually uses when referring to capital. Unlike habitus, it is external rather than internal to the self. It is of the order of what I have rather than what I am (in the way we differentiated between the two earlier in the chapter on habitus)." But this route will be quickly cut short for us, for Bourdieu never hesitates to inform us that while cultural capital can be a possession, it also comes in an "embodied" or "incorporated" state. As we are informed in his notable "Forms of Capital," capital "is accumulated labor (in its materialized form or its 'incorporated,' embodied form) which, when appropriated on a private, i.e., exclusive, basis by agents or groups of agents, enables them to appropriate social energy in the form of reified or living labor."[18] Later in that same essay we are told, "The accumulation of cultural capital in the embodied state, i.e., in the form of what is called culture, cultivation, *Bildung*, presupposes a process of embodiment, incorporation, which, insofar as it implies a labor of inculcation and assimilation, costs time, time which must be invested personally by the investor."[19]

Thus, there is no escaping the question: What is the difference between cultural capital and habitus? Strangely, sometimes Bourdieu himself explicitly states that there are no differences: "Cultural capital is a 'having' that has become a 'being,' a possession made bodily, having become an integral part of the 'person,' a habitus."[20]

Unfortunately, to make things even more difficult for readers, the same can be said of capital and *illusio*. In the passage from *Invitation to Reflexive Sociology* quoted earlier, we passed too quickly over a brief phrase inserted there: "capital is what is efficacious in a given field, both as a weapon and *as a stake* of struggle."[21] This is hardly the only place where capital makes its appearance in Bourdieu's work as "a stake in the game." As with *illusio*, it is conceived as a central pursuit that gives meaning to life and which by being shared—that is, the extent to which it is a *collusio*—ends up structuring the social spaces that Bourdieu calls "the field": "*A capital does not exist and function except in relation to a field.* It confers a power over the field, over the materialized or embodied instruments of production or reproduction whose distribution constitutes the very structure of the field, and over the regularities and the rules which define the ordinary functioning of the field, and thereby over the profits engendered in it."[22]

Capital, here, is in a number of ways micro-, objectified, *illusios*. There are as many capitals as there are fields of accumulation structured around specific interests. And these interests work as major and minor *illusios*. The general idea is this: If one is invested in being a carpenter, one becomes entangled with other people invested in being carpenters inside a competitive field structured by the struggle to define and to accumulate "carpentry capital" (note that it is not just about being a carpenter, since there are people who are carpenters without being invested in being carpenters). There will also be all kinds of subcapital. That is, what one actually accumulates in order to accumulate "carpentry capital" varies: It can be the amazing tools that one shows off, it can be the van that one drives, it can be the knowledge and the skills that one has, and it can be a certain mode of relating to and talking about timber. It can even be a certain attitude to life that derives a certain philosophy from relating to timber in a certain spiritual, mystical, or down to earth way. All of these are capitals and *illusios*.

Capital, then, is what people are after and the "object" toward which the social libido, which I described in chapter 3 as being associated with the *illusio*, is directed. Its structuring power over social life—or, more specifically, over social "fields"—comes from the different quantitative and qualitative degrees of success that people have in acquiring it. This ends up cementing itself into relations of power between those who have more capital and those who have less. Insofar as it is the object of yearning, desire, and pursuit, it belongs to the economy of the production, circulation, and accumulation of "meanings of life" that we analyzed in relation to the *illusio*. Louis Pinto—who was part of Bourdieu's research team at the École des Hautes Etudes en Sciences Sociales—in fact explicitly calls it "le capital des raisons d'exister."[23] And here again we are left with the same question we asked regarding habitus: Is there a difference between *illusio* and capital? I want to suggest that depending on what dimension of capital we are talking about, there is and there is not.

Capital as Possession, Capital as the Stake of the Game, and Capital as Recognition

Let us look closely at a classical paragraph where Bourdieu is listing the various forms of capital, defining them as forms of "social power": "These fundamental social powers are, according to my empirical investigations, firstly economic capital, in its various kinds; secondly cultural capital . . . again in its different kinds; and thirdly two forms of capital that are very strongly correlated, social capital, which consists of resources based on connections and group membership, and symbolic capital, which is the form the different types of capital take once they are perceived and recognized as legitimate."[24]

The classification used in this paragraph is rather peculiar, as the various forms of capital do not belong to the same order and are not of the same type. It is not equal to that "certain Chinese encyclopedia" made famous by Michel Foucault via Jorge Luis Borges,[25] but still, we have something like capital can be divided into *a* and *b*, and two other related forms, *c* and *d*. Though *d* is really *a*, *b*, and *c* in a different form. On the one hand, we have economic and cultural capital, and, on the other, we have the "correlated" social and symbolic capital. But symbolic capital is not just another capital of the same order. Rather, it is the form taken by economic, cultural, and social capital in some circumstances.

Let us leave aside the supposed kinship between social and symbolic capital for a while and concentrate on the divide between the first three capitals, on the one hand, and the last one, on the other. What is at stake in such a division is made quite explicit. Economic, cultural, and social capital are declared "social powers." But in some circumstances they become more than cultural power, economic power, and social power. They become a form of symbolic power. In the paragraph above, Bourdieu refers to this symbolic power as a new form of capital: symbolic capital. But throughout his work he is struggling with the conceptualization: Is the symbolic a form of capital, a type of capital, or a dimension of capital? Even in his later works, such as *Pascalian Meditations*, Bourdieu is still struggling to give this symbolic domain a rigorous formulation: "Every kind of capital (economic, cultural, social) tends (to different degrees) to function as symbolic capital (so that it might be better to speak, in rigorous terms, of the *symbolic effects of capital*) when it obtains explicit or practical recognition."[26]

I will stick with symbolic capital in this chapter. But regardless of the formulation, what is important is that the transformation of the economic, cultural, and social into symbolic occurs when the latter are no longer only social powers but social powers that are "perceived and recognized as legitimate."[27]

The nature of this difference is more complex than what meets the eye. In the first instance, when a capital is declared to be a social power, the relation that is of central significance is between the social agent and the capital. This relation is implicitly a binary relation of possession. The social agent comes to possess a certain amount of economic, cultural, or social capital, and this possession augments the social agent's capacity to act in the world according to how much they possess.

In the case of symbolic capital, and for symbolic capital to yield its specific form of symbolic power, more than a binary relation of possession is required. Here, the relation is between three, not just two, parties. To be sure, the relation is still present between the capital and the agent that possesses it. But a third party is introduced: an entity doing the work of recognition and legitimization. As Bourdieu puts it, "Symbolic capital is any property (and form of capital whether physical, economic, cultural or social) when it is perceived by social agents endowed with categories of perception which cause them to know it and to recognize it, to give it value."[28]

Here the power of the capital is not conferred by its efficiency but by the degree of recognition it gets from others for its efficient usage. It is one thing to say, "I am very good at playing piano" (i.e., a person has the cultural capital and the know-how to play piano). It is another to be recognized as "good at playing piano," which is where a person's cultural capital becomes another form of capital—symbolic capital. There are people who are happy with their degree of efficiency but who get no recognition for what they achieve (the people who get public recognition for an achievement that they themselves know is a mediocre achievement), but there are also cases of people who both are efficient and derive a sense of augmentation of being from their own sense of efficiency and equally derive a sense of augmentation of being from the recognition they get for their efficiency.

It is the same with *illusio*. *Illusio* is primarily a belief in the path one is taking in life and a sense of satisfaction derived from taking it. Yet this is different from the satisfaction one gets from the value of the path we take being recognized by others. Again, there are many situations where one embarks on a path that gives one public recognition but a path that leaves one deeply dissatisfied with oneself. Likewise, there are many situations where the reverse is true: people who are deeply satisfied with the path they have embarked on, a path that gives them fulfillment and a sense of raison d'être, but a path whose legitimacy and value is questioned by others. There is, then, a certain degree of narcissism as far as *illusio* is concerned: it is about the extent to which one is satisfied with oneself. When this path functions as capital, the derived satisfaction is longer as narcissistic and becomes dependent on the valorization of others.

From all of the above we can say that capital is articulated to the three dimensions of the political economy of being. In the first instance, it is a *possession*: It is the possession of a social power that enhances the social agents' capacity to practice. This makes capital articulated to the political economy of efficiency to which habitus belongs. In the second instance, capital is a *stake*: It is something that one pursues—or, better still, something that is considered worthy of investing one's life pursuing—and, in the process, something that gives our lives purpose and meaning. This makes capital articulated to the political economy of the meaningfulness of life to which *illusio* belongs. Finally, capital is articulated to its own *political economy of being*: It is a political economy in which the augmentation of being and viability is associated with the augmentation of recognition and legitimacy. We move from under the shadows of the energetics of Benedict de Spinoza and the existential problematics of Edmund Husserl to come under the shadow of the intersubjective problematics of G. W. F. Hegel. Just as, for Hegel, "self-consciousness achieves its satisfaction only in another self-consciousness," for Bourdieu, "Symbolic capital exists by and for perception or, more precisely, by and for those who perceive it and who can perceive it and make it exist as such only because they are endowed with adequate categories of perception."[29]

Recognition as Distinction and Legitimacy

Reading through Bourdieu's work there is little doubt about the importance of this association between an economy of viability and an economy of recognition. Sometimes one even gets the impression that the struggle for viability is before all else a struggle for recognition. As the quote already featured in the introduction to this book asserts, "there is no worse dispossession, no worse privation, perhaps, than that of the losers in the symbolic struggle for recognition, for access to a socially recognized social being, in a word, to humanity."[30]

There is, however, an important distinction between two facets of recognition that is not highlighted enough. This has to do with the struggle for recognition as a struggle for distinction and the struggle for recognition as a struggle for legitimacy. The difference between the two is particularly important from the perspective of an economy of being. It involves two different dimensions of viability: the accumulation of distinction is the accumulation of uniqueness, and the accumulation of legitimacy is the accumulation of social validity and authority. The first allows one to shine, and the second gives one the power to shape the world in one's own image. "The social world is both the product and the stake of inseparably cognitive and political symbolic struggles over knowledge and recognition, in which each pursues not only the imposition of an advantageous representation of himself or herself, with the strategies of 'presentation of self' so admirably analysed by [Erving] Goffman, but also the power to impose as legitimate the principles of construction of social reality most favourable to his or her social being (individual and collective, with, for example, struggles over the boundaries of groups) and to the accumulation of a symbolic capital of recognition."[31]

Before all else, the accumulation of distinction is the avoidance of seriality. Let's take the example of fashion, where the struggle for distinction is easy to visualize and exemplify. When I accumulate fashion I am hoping to come across as spunky. I am invested in looking fashionable. I go about learning what constitutes fashionable clothes in any given period and how these clothes are worn and where to buy them, as well as mixing with the people who wear them and internalizing the various strategies they use when wearing them. I might look at a fashion magazine and say, "This magazine has just come out today. I like this jacket and these pants featured on the front cover. I am going to go and buy them and wear them to a dinner party tonight." You can imagine that I won't go very far with this. If I am to appear at the dinner party wearing exactly what has been portrayed as very fashionable and chic on the front cover of the magazine this morning, I'd be as unfashionable as can be in the eyes of those who have seen the magazine, and in the eyes of everyone who will know what I have done. Why? Because I have lacked *distinction*. The accumulation of distinction cannot be achieved through pure mimicry. One needs to know how to add a distinctive trait that makes one stand out—what Bourdieu refers to as "distinctive power."[32] It is when people recognize in me a distinguishing trait that stands out that I can be said to be accumulating distinction. In this sense, the accumulation of distinction has all the marks of what we can refer to, from a Lacanian perspective, as a phallic modality of being. While Bourdieu himself does not speak of it in this way, I find it illuminating to do so. It allows a more explicit analytics of the augmentation of being associated with symbolic capital that is implicitly present in Bourdieu.[33]

A phallic modality of being is referred to as such after Sigmund Freud's theorization of penis envy. As is well known, for Freud penis envy refers to a phase in the development of female sexuality that coincides with the girls' realization that boys have something that they don't have: a penis.[34] For Freud, the envy cannot be explained without the basic psychoanalytic premise of a primordial lack: the idea that the moment humans develop consciousness they develop a sense that something is missing that stops them from experiencing a sentiment of total fulfillment. This feeling of lack and fragmentation is internal—that is, it is generated through an inward gaze at ourselves. When gazing at others from the outside, they generally appear as far more together than we are. In that sense, for Freud, and a point particularly developed by Jacques Lacan, the envy of the penis is the envy of what is believed to be behind the imagined fulfillment and togetherness of the other. This is important for understanding what is being said about symbolic capital and distinction here: the penis, in itself, has no value. Its value is that it is, at the most superficial level, protruding. It is a mark of distinction. This is why for Lacan there is no reason at all why the penis has to be the mark of distinction and have a phallic function.[35] Anything that is a mark of difference can have such a function. A boy with short hair can desire the long hair of a girl, and the hair thus becomes the phallus. What is crucial is that something only gains its importance by being desired, not because it has an intrinsic importance.

You can tear a little bit of plastic from a bag and throw it to two toddlers on the ground. One of them spots it and goes for it, aiming to grab it. As soon as the first toddler does that, the other toddler sees them going for it and will go for it too. As the second toddler races to get it first, the first toddler will think, "Ah, it must be important, because they are going for it. I'd better rush and grab it." This makes the second toddler think, "Ah, they are rushing to get it, I'd better really rush." And suddenly you have a dynamic where everyone wants *it*, thinking that having it is the most important thing in the world. It is in that sense that we say that the possession of symbolic capital as a mark of distinction institutes a phallic modality of being. It does so because it involves the possession of a valuable mark of distinction that is only valuable because the other desires it. As Bourdieu puts in the language of the time that Ferdinand de Saussure originally deployed, the value of capital, like that of the signifier, is *arbitrary*.[36]

For Freud, as for Lacan later, the possession of the phallus institutes two psychological dramas. Both are important to understand the struggle over symbolic capital. The first is the drama of those who do not have the phallus and who think that having it will bring fulfillment; as I have already noted, Freud associates this with the drama of feminine sexuality. The second, associated with masculine sexuality, is the drama of those who have the phallus. The possessors of the phallus have to contend with two contradictory sentiments: On the one hand, they are invited by those desiring what they possesses to believe that they have something important. But, on the other hand, they are no different than any other lacking subject; they experience themselves as lacking. Consequently, they are left with a particular kind of anxiety. For Freud and Lacan, this is the anxiety associated with the castration complex.[37] The possession of the phallus is always a fragile and paranoid possession; it involves a continual need to have this possession celebrated and appreciated, while at the same time involving a continual doubt regarding the value of what one possesses. This is what the phallic modality of being entails as far as the struggle over symbolic capital is a struggle for distinction.[38]

This phallic dimension is present, though not as dominant, when the struggle for recognition is primarily concerned with legitimacy. Here, as I have noted, recognition is not only about the recognition of one's uniqueness but about one's authority and social clout, or what Bourdieu refers to as social "weight."[39] As he put it, "the weight of different agents depends on their symbolic capital, i.e. on the *recognition*, institutionalized or not, that they receive from a group."[40]

To be considered legitimate is to have your personal views and interests considered to be *the* views and interests of the collective that is recognizing you. Legitimacy works through a reciprocal effect. To be considered legitimate is to be given the power to legitimize. It transforms your *illusio* into a *collusio*. In this sense, as Bourdieu puts it, "symbolic capital is a credit, it is the power granted to those who have obtained sufficient recognition to be in a position to impose recognition."[41] As such, one's symbolic capital is proportional to one's degree of legitimacy, which is in turn proportional to one's power to legitimize: "In the struggle for the imposition of the legitimate vision of the social world, . . . agents wield a power which is proportional to their symbolic capital, that is, to the recognition they receive from a group."[42]

Notably, with this facet of symbolic capital we return to a conception of viability associated with efficiency. But here it is an efficiency in the form of impact. The more symbolic capital social agents possess, the more their views matter, and the more they are empowered to shape reality. Symbolic capital gives the social agent the "power of nomination and of imposition of the legitimate principle of vision and division, universally recognized in a determinate social space."[43] And, as Bourdieu would have it, "What game is more vital, more total, than the symbolic struggle of all against all in which what is at stake is the power of *naming*, or categorization, in which everyone has stakes in his being, his values, the idea he has of himself?"[44]

All three of Pierre Bourdieu's analytical concepts that we have examined so far presuppose a social context that gives them their power and their meaning. Indeed, as I highlighted in chapter 1, the very concept of a habitual practice is only meaningful insofar as it is understood as a particular relation to the social. To use but one obvious example, there is no "habituated efficiency" in the abstract. It means little, as far as efficient swimming goes, to be an efficient swimmer in a nonswimming environment. A practice acquires its meaningfulness, its efficiency, and the recognition that it yields within specific social milieus. *Field* is the term Bourdieu uses to refer to and analyze this social milieu. As he puts it in the case of habitus, "The dispositions constituting the cultivated habitus are only formed, only function and are only valid in a field, in the relationship with a field. . . . This is why the same practices may receive opposite meanings and values in different fields, in different configurations or in opposing sectors of the same field."[1]

Throughout this book, I have been interested in exposing the anthropological underpinnings of Bourdieu's political economy of being. As such, in the first three chapters I presented habitus and *illusio* as primarily socioanthropological concepts. This is in the sense of them being concepts concerned with an analytics of the nature of humans inasmuch as they are social agents: how they are historically constituted as entities driven to augment their social being, and what properties they have that enhance our understanding of the way they engage in this pursuit. In chapter 4, I treated capital in much the same way. I highlighted the way it points to a conception of social subjects as driven by the desire to augment their being through the augmentation of their social recognition. *Field* is somewhat different, as it is a concept that presents itself primarily as sociological: It offers a theory of the nature of the social world and how to analyze it. From the perspective developed in this book, we can say that field is, before anything else, the very social space where a political economy of being unfolds—where the production and distribution of, and the struggle for, particular forms of "being" and "viability" unfold.[2]

But the division between the anthropological and the sociological, like most analytical divisions, is never neat. We saw, for instance, in chapter 1 how Bourdieu's habituated practical social agent does not sit outside the social world as a separate entity that interacts with it a posteriori but is ontologically constitutive of it. As such, just as all of Bourdieu's anthropological categories have a necessary sociological dimension, his sociological categories also have an anthropological dimension. Indeed, as I will argue in this chapter, while field points to a primarily sociological reality, it nonetheless also adds a further anthropological dimension to the political economy of being we are delineating: It points to and contributes to a particular experience of being as an experience of socioexistential mobility.

Field as an Analytical Concept

At its most basic, a field is the assemblage of people, objects, spaces, institutions, and social relations that are formed by people who enter the game of life by sharing similar interests. In society there are as many "specialized and relatively autonomous" fields as there are "stakes and interests."[3] As has been made clear in many introductions to the notion of field,[4] there is no doubt that Bourdieu aimed to use it to differentiate his work from certain Marxist models of the social, in which noneconomic domains of life were seen as "determined" by the economic structure of society. As he has put it,

> I hope to be able one day to demonstrate, everything leads us to suppose that far from being the founding model, the economic theory of the field is a particular case of the general theory of fields which is gradually being constructed by a sort of theoretical induction that is empirically validated, and which, while allowing us to understand the fecundity and the limits of the validity of transfers such as the one [Max] Weber effected, obliges us to rethink the presuppositions of economic theory, especially in the light of what is learned from the analysis of fields of cultural production.[5]

Yet this was never the only or the main issue the concept aimed to deal with. Another key problematic was a historical one. For Bourdieu, the existence of a society made out of a multiplicity of specialized and relatively autonomous fields is not something true of all societies at all times. It is a particularly modern phenomenon that at best existed in a much less pronounced form in the premodern era.[6]

When Marcel Mauss analyzed extramodern gift-based societies, he highlighted what was for him a crucial point: a gift differs from a commodity not only in the way it functions as an economic category. As important, the commodity is mainly an economic category, while the gift was what Mauss famously called a "total social fact."[7] Part of what he meant was that gift exchange had, at the same time, an economic, a political, a spiritual, an affective dimension, and so on, while the buying of a commodity, as a relation between buyer and seller, was far more unidimensionally economic. A commodity can only come about as a result of a historical process in which the various interests and dimensions of life that were fused to the point of being indistinguishable in extramodern relations, such as gift relations, become increasingly differentiated.[8] A theory of fields is necessary to account for this differentiation. Bourdieu has in mind both the processes of institutional separation, such as the separation of religion from the state or of economic institutions from the domain of leisure, and the circulation of ideas in everyday life about the different logics and the different social and emotional investments that govern separate spheres of life, such as in the saying "Family is family and business is business."[9] As such, social being itself becomes fragmented into *economic being*, *spiritual being*, and the like. Field, then, is an analytics of society as an articulation of the multiplicity of spaces where struggles for the augmentation of these particularized forms of being are occurring.

To say that *field* is an analytical concept is to say that it is produced by social scientists for the purpose of analyzing society. Generally speaking, people do not go around talking about being positioned in fields. In that sense, *field* is an etic category. It is similar to, and does the same kind of work as, habitus. But, as I discussed in chapter 2, *habitus* can refer both to realities that are not available in practice, such as "structuring structures," and to realities such as "practical sense" and "inclinations" that are practically experienced by social agents, and as such have a particular way of existing and being spoken about in people's everyday lives. As I have argued, while people don't go around talking about having—let alone about being—a habitus, they nonetheless have a sense of some elements of the reality that habitus tries to capture scientifically. They might say, "That's how these people, x, are; it is in their nature to do y when confronted with the situation z." Or, "They've always felt more at home in this rather than that environment." Or, "In situation y, she can't help but do z." People might also use semitheoretical categories associated with "character" or "personality." In the same way, *field*, as we shall see, points to a structural reality that is not experienced in everyday life and also to the social space that people imagine themselves to exist in. As social agents we get a sense of the spaces where people are into whatever we are into. (I have a sense of the people who are interested in the work of Bourdieu at the very moment I am writing this and, as such, have an inkling of a field of Bourdieu studies.) We also have an imaginary of the collective of people we want to impress when performing a social action. We can say to someone, "I don't care what so-and-so thinks of what I am doing; the people I care about are x." In such instances field is a scientific category aiming to account for the properties of the social space that people experience it as possessing. It aims to be more rigorous and more probing and to have more explanatory power than the categories that laypeople have, but it remains concerned with the realities that people create through their practices. At the same time, however, it is also a scientific category that brings out a dimension of the social world that is only available to social scientists as people with a particular perspective and interest in the world. As with habitus, the scientific language Bourdieu uses is structuralist.[10] After all, field is the "structure" that is structured by and that structures the "structured structure that is predisposed to function as a structuring structure." I hope to show that there are important insights to gain beyond this admittedly comical tautology. At this stage, I simply want to highlight that it is because Bourdieu's categories continuously move between these different perspectives and dimensions that his analytics can oscillate between the observable and the unobservable, the structural and the phenomenological, and, as we shall see, the scientific and the political.

In an important way, the concept of *field* offers a certain complexification of Émile Durkheim's notion of society while keeping to his ontological claims about the nature of the social as a *sui generis* reality: A field is the product of human practices and yet, at the same time, like all "social facts," it is a different order of reality from the individuals and the practices that constitute it. This, as we shall see, is where the most original innovations to the analysis of the political economy of being are formulated. But it is important, nonetheless, to recognize that all the Durkheimian chicken-and-egg mental gymnastics that social analysts engage in to account for the relation between people and society apply to the relation between social agents and fields. Thus, a field is seen from one perspective to be dependent on the social subjects that create it, while from another it preexists them. A field is seen as shaped by the social agent's struggles that make it into what it is, but social agents are also seen as shaped by the fields, and the social locations within those fields, that they find themselves in when they come into existence. There is no need to go further into the gains and the difficulties that emanate from this dimension of field analysis, as more than enough has been written about it. What I want to do in this chapter is take what I have covered so far to help point us to some of the specificities of field insofar as it is a space that is both created by a political economy of being and the space where this political economy unfolds. I will first examine the more straightforward conception of field as a space of practices centered on the production and distribution of and struggles over particular forms of being. Then I will examine the more complex conception of the field as an active generator of socioexistential forces.

Field as a Space of Shared Interests

As noted above, a field operates first and foremost as a description of a space of practices where people are actively involved in the production and pursuit of specific interests. People who share similar interests are people who derive the viability of their lives from similar pursuits. They share similar conceptions of what makes life worthwhile. That is, they share a similar *illusio*.[11] Interest and *illusio* are interchangeable. When speaking of interest, Bourdieu uses the same strong, affective, and existential sense of interest that defines *illusio*: "Interest is at once a condition of the functioning of a field (a scientific field, the field of *haute couture*, etc.), in so far as it is what 'gets people moving,' what makes them get together, compete and struggle with each other, and a product of the way the field functions."[12]

Interest, then, like *illusio*, is a provider of raisons d'être. It is what "gets people moving." For Bourdieu, to invest oneself in a specific interest is to invest in what propels us in the world. It is an investment that involves putting the viability of one's life on the line, whether the latter is experienced as one's "honor," "future," or "well-being," or in any of the many other ways in which people speak of their life in general. Thus, to give an example, it is not enough to be a carpenter to belong to a field of carpentry. To belong to the field, you have to have an existential investment in being a carpenter—something in the form of an "unquestionable belief in the importance of carpentry"—for your life to be meaningful. As Bourdieu puts it in *Pascalian Meditations*,

All those who are involved in the fields, whether champions of orthodoxy or heterodoxy, share a tacit adherence to the same *doxa* which makes their competition possible and assigns its limits (the heretic remains a believer who preaches a return to purer forms of the faith). It effectively forbids questioning of the principles of belief, which would threaten the very existence of the field. Participants have ultimately no answer to questions about the reasons for their membership in the game, their visceral commitment to it; and the principles which may be invoked in such a case are merely *post festum* rationalizations intended to justify an unjustifiable investment, to themselves as much as to others.[13]

To stay with the above example, to belong to the field of carpentry the field has to *seriously and unquestionably* matter to you such that it moves you to accumulate "carpentry capital" in some form or another. In so doing, you both join the field of carpentry and participate in making it what it is. A field is thus structured around shared *illusios* and the pursuit of capital associated with those *illusios*. Within a field people are accumulating specific capitals, struggling to valorize the capitals that they have, contesting the value of the capitals that others have, and so on. People aim for power and domination not because power and domination are what they seek but because power and domination are the means of ensuring that it is their conception of the viable life that prevails.

As this makes clear, the fact that people share a similar conception of the viable life does not make a field a harmonious community of believers. It makes it a space of struggle. For "it tends to be forgotten that a fight presupposes agreement between the antagonists about what it is that is worth fighting about."[14] Indeed, there is "an objective complicity which underlies all the antagonisms. . . . [T]hose points of agreement are held at the level of what 'goes without saying,' they are left in the state of doxa, in other words everything that makes the field itself, the game, the stakes, all the presuppositions that one tacitly and even unwittingly accepts by the mere fact of playing, of entering into the game."[15] Thus Bourdieu argues that "the scientific field is an armed struggle among adversaries." Nonetheless, the scientists participating in the field have also a collective interest in the value of "the weapons," meaning the forms of capital, that they use to fight among each other. For the "power and effectiveness" of these weapons "rises with the scientific capital collectively accumulated in and by the field."[16]

As important as understanding the nature of the "interests" that gather the "interested" social subjects around them, generate struggles, and get a field moving is the way social subjects become interested in and captured by the field. For Bourdieu, the strong existential attachment that marks this interest is not a matter of mere will but a mode of having particular dispositions that inclines the social agents to be "sucked into the field." As Bourdieu puts it, "one cannot enter this magic circle by an instantaneous decision of the will, but only by birth or by a slow process of co-option and initiation which is equivalent to a second birth."[17] This process is affected by the location that social agents find themselves in as they come into being in the field. This location is marked by the kind of past, as an inheritance of already accumulated capitals, and the kind of future, in the form of a path for self-realization, it offers the social agent. It highlights the nature of the field as a space for the distribution of being. Here, rather than being imagined as spaces of struggle, fields are perceived as spaces of social determination. The two are of course related, but it is important to recognize them as separate conceptual components that work together to make *field* do the analytical work it does.

When seen as spaces where people come together around shared life pursuits, and where they struggle against each other to define and accumulate the capitals that constitute and are constituted by those pursuits, fields are imagined as inert and undifferentiated backgrounds where the action is unfolding. To see them as spaces of social determination invites a different imaginary spatial topography. Here they are perceived to be marked by the unequal distribution of capitals that weigh differently on the social agents positioned within them. Likewise, certain future paths are already carved into them. These are what Bourdieu calls "spaces of possibility." They invite those social agents who feel inclined to take them to do so and to embark on their journeys of self-realization. As such, rather than being a mere inert background, fields are seen to exert an active pressure on those positioned within them. As Bourdieu argues, against a Cartesian conception of a passive nature, the notion of fields participates in a dynamic vision that grants both the social and the natural world "a capacity to act specific to them."[18]

Nonetheless, this active conception of fields in the political economy of being does not introduce us to a new dimension of what social being entails. The latter remains defined within the confines captured by habitus, *illusio*, and capital: being as complicity with the world, being as raison d'être, and being as recognition. Fields only work to affect the production and distribution of those forms of social being. This changes with the conceptualization of fields as "structures."

Field as Structure

At first sight, field presents itself as a structure in the way most sociologies of power understand structure: an enduring relation between dominant and dominated groups or classes. The struggles for the meaning and for the accumulation of certain capital within a field ensure that some social agents end up in a dominant position by being able to impose and valorize their own conception of being and viability—their own capital—over the field and by accumulating more of that capital. By the same token, people with less valorized capital or merely less capital find themselves in a dominated position. As is always the case, to be dominant not only means to be in a hierarchically superior position but to have the power to maintain oneself in such a position. The power to dominate and the power to reproduce one's domination are one and the same. It is in such a process where relations of power endure that the social world becomes structured by them. Field aims to account for both the way the existing structure of enduring relations of power and the struggle to maintain or transform those relations go hand in hand. As Bourdieu writes,

> The structure is not immutable, and the topology that describes a state of the social positions permits a dynamic analysis of the conservation and transformation of the structure of the active properties' distribution and thus of the social space itself. That is what I mean when I describe the global social space as a *field*, that is, both as a field of forces, whose necessity is imposed on agents who are engaged in it, and as a field of struggles within which agents confront each other, with differentiated means and ends according to their position in the structure of the field of forces, thus contributing to conserving or transforming its structure.[19]

Nonetheless, it is important to highlight that, for Bourdieu, structure does not mean an enduring interactional relation. This is where the Durkheimian ontology of seeing social facts as real, *sui generis*, which I referred to in chapter 1, becomes particularly important. A structured interaction is still an interaction between agents and, as such, is a different reality from the structure created by those interactions, which is a relational reality in and of itself. As Bourdieu notes,

> By contrast with the interactionist vision, which knows no other form of social efficacy than the "influence" directly exerted by one enterprise (or person entrusted with representing it) over another through some form of "interaction," the structural vision takes account of effects that occur outside of any interaction: the structure of the field, defined by the unequal distribution of capital, that is, the specific weapons (or strengths), weighs, quite apart from any direct intervention or manipulation, on all the agents engaged in the field; and the worse placed they are within that distribution, the more it restricts the *space of possibles* open to them. The dominant is the one that occupies a position in the structure such that the structure acts on its behalf.[20]

Here structure is conceived as a "deep" structure that lies beyond the realm of visibility of the social agents, undergirding interactive reality. In fact, it works as a generative mechanism that plays a causal role in making observable social reality what it is. The idea of field as a structure of society is similar to the idea of habitus as a structure of the social agent. It is useful to go back to chapter 2's section, "A Generative Mechanism, Part 1: An Inner Causal Structure," to be reminded of what such a critical realist conception of structure entails ontologically. Bourdieu makes this clear, in fact—perhaps clearer than when talking about habitus as structure:

> Thinking in terms of a field requires a conversion of one's entire usual vision of the social world, a vision is interested only in those things which are visible: in the individual, the *ens realissimum* to which a sort of fundamental ideological interest attaches us; in the group, which is only apparently defined by the mere relations, temporary or enduring, informal or institutionalized, obtaining between its members; or even in relations understood as *interactions*, that is, as concretely enacted intersubjective relations. In fact, just as the Newtonian theory of gravitation could be developed only by breaking away from Cartesian realism, which refused to recognize any mode of physical action other than shock and direct contact, in the same way, the notion of field presupposes that one break away from the realist representation which leads one to reduce the effect of the milieu

to the effect of the direct action that takes place in any interaction. It is the structure of the constitutive relations of the space of the field which determines the forms that can be assumed by the visible relations of interaction and the very content of the experience that agents may have of them.[21]

A first step in moving away from thinking of the structure as structured interaction is to think of it as a relation between enduring differentials in the distributions of capital and not differences and relations between the people who inherit that capital—or, at least, to highlight the relation between agents as embodiments of the relation between differentials of capital. Thus, in *The Social Structures of the Economy*, Bourdieu argues that it is "the firms, defined by the volume and structure of specific capital they possess, that determine the structure of the field that determines them, for example, the state of the forces exerted on the whole set of firms engaged in the production of similar goods."[22] But the most general definition of the field as a structural reality abstracts from the social agents altogether, as this well-known passage makes clear: "The social world can be conceived as a multidimensional space that can be constructed empirically by discovering the main factors of differentiation which account for the differences observed in a given social universe. . . . It follows that the structure of this space is given by the distribution of the various forms of capital, that is, by the distribution of the properties which are active within the universe under study—those properties capable of conferring strength, power and consequently profit on their holder."[23]

As can be seen here, to get to the significance of this notion of structure, it is not enough to substitute the relation between forms of capital for the relation between agents. It is also important to highlight the idea of capitals having *properties* and *powers*, for it is the relation between these properties that is being highlighted and that gives fields their dynamic specificities. Here Bourdieu is inspired by Gaston Bachelard, who speaks of the magnetic field as a "field of possible forces."[24] It is why Bourdieu often speaks of "fields of forces" and of "effects of fields." Thus, "We may think of a field as a space within which an effect of field is exercised, so that what happens to any object that traverses this space cannot be explained solely by the intrinsic properties of the object in question."[25] A field is not only a relation between forms of capital as forces, then; it also generates its own forces, but does so *precisely because* it is the relation between forces and powers. Consequently, those who are positioned in the field are not only subjected to the powers of those they are opposed to or the powers of the capital that is at their disposition, but also have to contend with the autonomous forces of the field. Talking about the field of power, Bourdieu describes it as "a field of latent, potential forces which play upon any particle which may venture into it."[26]

In an interview, while talking about the intellectual field, Bourdieu states,

> When I talk of intellectual field, I know very well that in this field I will find "particles" (let me pretend for a moment that we are dealing with a physical field) that are under the sway of forces of attraction, of repulsion, and so on, as in a magnetic field. Having said this, as soon as I speak of a field, my attention fastens on the primacy of this system of objective relations over the particles themselves. And we could say, following the formula of a famous German physicist, that the individual, like the electron, is an *Ausgeburt des Felds*: he or she is in a sense an emanation of the field.[27]

This is the important thing to always retain: Field is not only a background, nor is it only active through the way it arranges the active forces present in the various habitus, *illusios,* and capitals that make it up. It generates its own forces that contribute to the making of social life.

In introducing this chapter, I argued that while field can be conceived as a sociological category that accounts for the social background or the social process through which the augmentation of being is unfolding, its more original dimension—as far as the latter process is concerned—is that it gives us another anthropological take on it. Yet as we have moved further into the structural nature of fields we seem to have moved further away from any anthropological or phenomenological concern and more into a world of social physics where terms such as *particles, magnetic fields,* and *potential and active forces* dominate. Rather than being concerned with any question of augmentation of being, Bourdieu appears to be more concerned with a kind of sociophysical movement of social agents and the forces that affect that movement. This language, as we shall see, extends further with such concepts as *trajectory, weight,* and *gravity.* Yet we are not as far from phenomenological concerns as we might think. Paradoxically, we can only fully understand the phenomenological dimension of this "social physics" by going further into the way Bourdieu conceives it.

The Socioexistential Physics of Fields

The idea of a "social physics" has been a haunting aspiration in the social sciences from the very moment of its emergence. It has been an aspiration because of the early positivist ambition of sociology to be a science on par with other sciences, and it has been haunting because of the gap between the ambition and sociology's actual capacity to partake in such positivism. Positivist social scientists are haunted by a form of "lack" when trying to conceive of social causality and formulate social laws; and, often enough, the rejection of positivist sociology also produces a ghostly effect by taking the form of an exorcism. That is, rather than confronting the tensions that arise from the very notion of social causality and social laws and treating those tensions themselves as productive analytical tools, some forms of antipositivism try to do away with the tension altogether and rid sociology of the very notion of "causality," thereby dismissing the very idea of a "social science." This is what paradoxically ends up giving "social physics" a ghostly presence even within interpretive sociology.

Bourdieu's conceptualization of practice, like most good sociologies, aims to combine insights from both traditions mentioned above rather than create rigid polarities between them. But it is also unique in the way it fuses an interpretive phenomenological approach where the emphasis is on "lived experience" without wanting to forgo the more "physicalist" approach that conceives of the social and of social agents in terms of causality, motion, and fields of forces. At the heart of this is what I have referred to as Bourdieu's ontological perspectivism, which does not differentiate between the social scientific point of view and the social agents' point of view in terms of objective and subjective but in terms of different dimensions of reality, whether physical or symbolic. "Social subjects comprehend the social world which comprehends them," he writes. "This means that they cannot be characterized simply in terms of material properties, starting with the body, which can be counted and measured like any other object in the physical world. In fact, each of these properties, be it the height or volume of the body or the extent of landed property, when perceived and appreciated in relation to other properties of the same class by agents equipped with socially constituted schemes of perception and appreciation, functions as a symbolic property."[28]

We can see here how one of the basic ideas of structuralism becomes the very principle of reality. This is the idea that a symbolic system is a system of differences and that each unit within this system has no intrinsic meaning or "value" in itself but gains its significance from the way it differentiates itself from other units within the system. Consequently, as Bourdieu goes on to say,

> social science does not have to choose between that form of social physics, represented by Durkheim . . . and the idealist semiology which, undertaking to construct "an account of accounts," as Harold Garfinkel puts it, can do no more than record the recordings of a social world which is ultimately no more than the product of mental, i.e., linguistic, structures. What we have to do is to bring into the science of scarcity, and of competition for scarce goods, the practical knowledge which the agents obtain for themselves by producing— on the basis of their experience of the distributions, itself dependent on their position in the distributions—divisions and classifications which are no less objective than those of the balance-sheets of social physics.[29]

Social space and modes of classification of social space are part of objective social reality because, as we shall further explore in this book's conclusion, the struggle over the world is the struggle over the classification of the world and, as such, a struggle over the very constitution of reality. Because of this, in Bourdieu's world *objectivist* reality is always conceived as entangled with *subjectivist* and experiential reality—so are the inert and the living, and the passive and the active. To capture this, Bourdieu often makes recourse to concepts that straddle these two dimensions and fuse them together.

Let's go back to the sentence, "Social subjects comprehend the social world which comprehends them." "Comprehend," here, is a good enough translation of the French verb *comprendre*, but it does not, perhaps, capture as well as the French word the dual objectivist and subjectivist nature of its signification. The first "comprehend" in the sentence refers to *comprendre*, which means "to understand," and is, of course, the mainstay of the *Verstehen* tradition.[30] The second "comprehend" directs us toward a more objectivist reality, as it means "to include" or "to encompass." This meaning is still present in the English word *comprehensive*. Thus, the objectivist fact of being comprehended (that is, encompassed in and captured by the world) goes hand in hand with the ability to comprehend (that is, to understand and capture the world). The relation is dialectical: The way we mentally encompass the world is constitutive of the way the world encompasses us, and vice versa.

A similar fusion is achieved with Bourdieu's usage of the concept *occupy*, as in the idea of social agents *occupying* a position in the field: *occuper* means "to occupy a position" in the social structure, and *être occuper* means "to be occupied" (or also *être préoccuper*, "to be preoccupied") with the world. This coupling of social location with existential concerns is also articulated to a coupling of the passive and the active in relation to the notion of "position" occupied. For Bourdieu, every position entails a mode of position-taking.[31] All social agents are "agents in motion" who follow a "class trajectory": they cannot understand where they are without understanding where they are going, which is related to both where the amount of capital they have inherited and accumulated is propelling them and where they are taking themselves according to their habitus and their *illusio*. This brings us back to the sociophysical movement of "social particles" in the field with which we started this section and whose articulation to phenomenological and existential concerns I hope we are now in a better position to understand. This is because the notion of movement, like the notions of "occupy" and the notion of "comprehend," denotes both a sociophysical and a phenomenological/existential dimension.

This is well illustrated in Bourdieu's conceptualization of the notion of trajectory, which emerged very early in Bourdieu's work and is developed in the 1966 article "Condition de classe et position de classe." There he explains that while class positions, measured in terms of amount of capital accumulated within a field, are important tools of analysis, in themselves they offer a deforming or static conception of social position and need to be understood in relation to a more dynamic conception of class trajectory. This is because a static concept of class location that is captured by what he calls a "synchronic cut" leaves out all of what "concretely defines the way the position is experienced as a mere stage in a process of social climbing or social decline."[32] Consequently, "it follows that one has to distinguish between the properties attached to the position as defined synchronically and the properties attached to the becoming of the position."[33]

In addition to this still largely objectivist conception of the relation between trajectory and class position, Bourdieu articulates a further important dimension. He argues that while it is important to capture a person or a group's class position in the social structure, one cannot assume that people passively occupy the class position in which their possession of a certain amount of capital places them. To see people on a trajectory is to also see them as capable of acting strategically within their class position. That is, along with class position one needs to examine the strategies of position-taking (*les prises de positions*) that social subjects engage in. As he explains in a 1974 article, "Avenir de classe et causalité du probable," "the capital effectively possessed *at a given moment* . . . is not enough to completely explain practices [emanating from a specific class location]. . . . If, in other words, certain categories of agents can overestimate their chances, and therefore really increase them, it is because the [social subject's] dispositions tend to reproduce not the position of which they are the product, caught at a certain period of time, but the *angle* [*la pente*]" in which this social position is located and which instills in social subjects their "dispositions with respect to the future."[34] That is, to sum up, the moment a social subject is positioned within the social field, they are propelled by their inheritance. This inheritance is not only a certain amount of cultural and economic capital associated with the class position one is born into. One also slowly inherits, mainly through the internalization of a familial ethos which is itself determined by class trajectory, a certain disposition toward the accumulation of capital—for instance, whether one is inclined to "furiously" accumulate capital or to "take it easy." This disposition is, as we have seen in chapter 1, an important component of habitus. Therefore, at any point, the class trajectory is given a further dynamic and direction by the process and modality of accumulation of capital that is emanating from the habitus.

But the driving force that animates this dynamic of capital inheritance and capital accumulation does not happen in a social void. Social subjects are not only endowed with a specific form of social motion related to class trajectory but are also subjected to the forces animating the social spaces they are traversing. These are the forces of the "social fields," as Bourdieu has theorized them. And it is here that we come to an important addition to the notion of movement. After complementing a passive conception of movement (movement as socially determined by factors such as social location and inheritance) with an active conception of movement (position-taking), Bourdieu articulates to this objectivist conception of movement an existential/vitalist conception that takes us into the domain of "what moves us," in the sense of what "concerns us" and "gets us going." The field, and particularly the central role of interests (those things that preoccupy us as we occupy the field), both instill in social agents an existential propelling mechanism: "Because we are always more or less caught up in one of the social games offered us by different fields, it does not occur to us to ask why there is action rather than nothing—which, unless one supposes a natural propensity for action or work, is not at all self-evident."[35] This "propensity for action" comes from the inseparably "economic and psychological investments" in the field. It is through these investments that the field becomes the space that "gets people moving."[36] It does so insofar as these investments are the mark of the seriousness with which social agents enter the field. They do so "exposed and endangered in the world, faced with the risk of emotion, lesion, suffering, sometimes death, and therefore obliged to take the world seriously."[37] This notion of seriousness puts us before one of Bourdieu's key categories: that of social gravity, which we have already encountered when examining *illusio*, but which takes on further importance when seen from the wider perspective of the field. It is a concept of a similar nature to *occupation* and *comprehension* in that it denotes both an objectivist meaning—the way the social forces of the world pull us into this world (gravity in the more Newtonian sense of the word)— and a subjectivist meaning (gravity as an indication of how seriously one takes the social world, as when we speak of "the gravity of the situation").

Social Physics and Social Gravity

Social gravity emerged as an irresistible concept in the early days of sociology, when it was common to fantasize social science as a "social physics." Historically, there have been two ways in which sociology as social physics has been conceived. The first approaches the issue from a largely epistemological perspective: It is interested in ways in which sociologists can formulate explanatory laws about social life, akin in terms of their scientific validity to those perceived to exist in physics. As is well known, this perspective has its roots in the work of Auguste Comte and his attempt to move both society itself, and reflections about the social, beyond what he sees as the "theologico-metaphysical" state where they have been mired, failing to move to the "positive" state where they become fully rational.[38] Thus, for Comte, what is at stake is "extending to social phenomena the spirit which governs the treatment of all other natural phenomena."[39] In this perspective, the notion of social gravity has been largely conceived in metaphoric terms. Such a usage was closer to the everyday, as well as the literary,[40] usages of gravity even though the social scientific metaphors aimed for a greater sense of exactitude and precision.

The second conception of sociology as social physics sees the relation as more of an ontological matter. Here the issue is not so much the "spirit" in which social laws are conceived and the way they can be compared to physical laws, but the extent to which physical laws themselves are relevant to understanding society. That is, this second approach is interested in the way people and societies constitute spatially positioned physical objects in themselves and are thus subjected to physical laws. In ways similar to sociobiology's interest in the biological basis of the social and the claims it makes concerning the relevance of this basis, this approach is also interested in the consequences of the "physicality" of the social and its relevance, as well as in the place of a sociophysics in a more general sociology.

This approach began in the 1830s with the Belgian astronomer Adolphe Quetelet, who saw himself as taking up Comte's challenge with a kind of Newtonian spirit, aimed at creating a "méchanique sociale." For, as he asked, "would it not be absurd to believe that while all else happens according to such admirable laws, the human species alone is left to blind abandon . . . ?"[41] In the United States, the first notion of social physics in line with this form of questioning was deployed by H. C. Carey, who saw "the great law of molecular gravitation as the *indispensable* condition of the existence of the being known as man."[42] His work was influential in the development of notions of social gravity among social geographers, some of whom tried to conceive of human interaction in social—urban and nonurban—space in ways similar to the interaction of heavenly bodies in Isaac Newton's universal law of gravitation. While most of these approaches are perceived to be naive today, the general spirit that animated them remains alive in many sociological works.

That general spirit remains present in Bourdieu's deployment of the concept. For him, social gravity is nothing other than the forces experienced by the social subject moving along its trajectory, meeting up with the social forces of the field that offers social subjects the opportunity of investing themselves in the social world of this field, and in this sense becoming the field. Once they do, they have invested their lives by taking a specific social path (and the *illusio* that comes with it) and, in a sense, from that moment onward, they subconsciously know that their life (in the sense of its very meaning and significance) is now on the line. Thus, the subject becomes aware of the "gravity" of the situation at the same time as society's social forces of gravity pull them to become an internalized part of that society. This is a common feeling for ethnographers: The more they interact with the social milieu they are analyzing (the field, in an anthropological sense), the more they become encompassed by the web of social relations that make up that field, the more they understand the social transactions occurring around them and, finally, the more it becomes difficult for them to extricate themselves from these webs of social relations.[43]

In Bourdieu's analysis of Gustave Flaubert's *L'éducation sentimentale*, which we briefly examined in chapter 3, we have a tale of six young men from various social backgrounds trying to make lives for themselves as they are drawn to and torn among the fields of power, money, and art. In this analysis, Bourdieu gives one of the most totalizing accounts of the way he perceives the working of the relation between class trajectory, habitus, field, *illusio,* and social gravity. He writes, "As if in some Leibnizian universe, everything is given *in actu*, from the outset, to the Godlike creator-spectator. The young men's trajectories and the different forms that love, money and power give to each one's sentimental education are all determined by the forces present in the field interacting with the embodied forces of the young men's habitus. In such a universe there is no room for chance."[44]

Thus, Bourdieu explains,

> *Education* may be read as an experimental novel in the true sense of the term. Flaubert first offers us a description of the field of power, within which he traces the movements of six young men, including Frédéric, who are propelled in it like so many particles in a magnetic field. And each one's trajectory—what we normally call the history of his life—is determined by the interaction between the forces of the field and his own inertia, that is, the habitus as the remanence of a trajectory which tends to orient future trajectory. The field of power is a field of latent, potential forces which play upon any particle which may venture into it, but it is also a battlefield which can be seen as a game. In this game, the trump cards are the habitus.[45]

Each of the social subjects—the young men—is looking in a sense to invest himself but, of all of them, as we saw in chapter 3, it is Frédéric who is the least decisive and the one unable to take a definite social path. Bourdieu sees the character of Frédéric as the one that demonstrates most fully all the implications of Flaubert's model—and, by implication, Bourdieu's own model, if there ever were an imaginary situation where it could be tested in laboratory-like conditions: "An heir who does not wish to be taken up by his inheritance and made what he is, i.e. a 'bourgeois,' he wavers between reproduction strategies which are all quite incompatible with one another . . . he vacillates between an artistic or a business career. . . .

This vacillation is the infallible sign of a being without gravity, lacking all the weight of character and seriousness, and incapable of offering the least resistance to the forces of the field."[46]

Social gravity is not only the way society pulls us to it and the way we experience the seriousness of life; it is also the only means we have to anchor ourselves in the social and to give stability and consistency to our world against "the lightness of being." In *Pascalian Meditations*, Bourdieu goes further, arguing that the chronically unemployed, by losing any sense of anchorage in the social, live in a world where reality begins to dissolve. Consistent with his "realist perspectivism," Bourdieu is saying that, without social gravity, people not only lose a sense of the meaning of their lives but the world itself loses its material consistency: time and space dissolve and we come closer to an experience of nothingness. While society is indeed the distributor of "meanings of life," these meanings only acquire their full intensity in the field the moment they allow social agents to start taking the world "seriously," with gravity. This very gravity of intent makes for the power of gravity as an experience of the intensity of the real—the reality of the real, one can meaningfully say, despite the awkwardness of the formulation. Thus, for Bourdieu, it is the very intensity of one's interest in the world that makes for the meaningfulness and intensity of the world as space and time. We are far more with Benedict de Spinoza than with Isaac Newton here.

Toward a Socioexistential Physics

That a viable life presupposes a sense that one is "going somewhere"—what I have called, inspired by Bourdieu, "existential mobility"—is something that I found particularly productive to think with in both my work on transnational Lebanese migration and my work on white racists in the West.[47] I found that both the migrants and the racists sought a sense of existential mobility and aimed to avoid its opposite, what I referred to as "stuckedness."

In the case of Lebanese immigrants, I took seriously their equation of well-being with a sense of mobility that is present in common everyday statements such as, "How are you going?" This allowed me to show how, in many instances, the Lebanese engaged in the physical form of mobility that we call migration because they were in search of existential mobility. This differs from the physical movement of tourists, for instance, whose physical mobility (travel) is part of their accumulation of existential mobility. I argued that one understood certain types of migration better if one saw the immigrants concerned as looking for a space that constitutes a suitable launching pad for their social and existential self.

Likewise, theorizing a kind of comparative existential mobility has allowed me a particular insight into certain specific forms of white racism marked by resentment and envy toward immigrants, as well as ethnic and racial minorities. When I was writing my manuscript on the subject in the late 1990s, there was a common belief, especially among cosmopolitan small-*l* liberals, that the racism toward immigrants of the followers of Pauline Hanson in Australia, like that of the followers of Marine Le Pen in France, is a working-class form of racism. I showed that this was not the case: Hansonite and Le Penist racism was primarily derived from a sense of "mobility envy" by people from all classes who felt they weren't moving "well enough." An example was white Australians resenting the presence of so many doctors of Indian heritage in their hospitals.

It is on the basis of observing patterns of behavior similar to the above that I have argued that, in Australia, there was a link between the racism toward Indigenous people and immigrants exhibited by the white racist Hansonites, and the latter's sense of stuckedness, which was generated not only by neoliberal globalization but also, in particular, by the insecurity in job tenure that has increased the sense of "being stuck in one's job" everywhere around the world.

I mention this not because it offers some "full-fledged" Bourdieusian analysis of the phenomena I am examining, but to exemplify where the kind of analytic imagination that sees in fields an analytics of socioexistential mobility can take us. But I think that Bourdieu's work in this regard can be further developed to go well beyond a simple duality between existential mobility and existential "stuckedness." I believe that he provides the basis for an entire existential physics that can generate an even more refined analytics of how well and to what extent people move socially and existentially. One important variable in this regard, and that I have only mentioned so far, is "social weight." Speaking of the firms that constitute the economic field, Bourdieu argues, "The weight (or energy) associated with an agent, which undergoes the effects of the field at the same time as it structures that field, depends on all the other points and the relations between all the points, that is to say, on the entire space."[48]

Again, one can do a lot with a notion of social and existential weight in this regard. Reading Bourdieu made me think differently about a particular incident that happened while conducting my ethnography with the Lebanese diaspora. I was leaving Beirut-Rafic Hariri International Airport bound for Paris with one of my informants, Wafa, and her mother. Her mother was carrying such a great deal of luggage—well beyond the allowed weight allocation—that it caused a scene at the airport. Wafa looked very embarrassed by the whole situation. She said to me that it was always like this traveling with her mother, and adding, "It's like traveling with someone who comes from the village."

Wafa had a clear sense of the class connotations of how much weight one carries when traveling: cosmopolitan people travel lightly, country people take too much luggage. But what interested me was the way her mother's luggage "weighed" on Wafa. Her mother was carrying the heavy physical luggage but was unaffected by it, symbolically or existentially. Wafa, on the other hand, because she saw herself through others' eyes (perhaps mine, on this occasion), was the one affected by it symbolically and existentially. What is interesting, from a Bourdieusian perspective, is that the notion of "existential weight" was not merely an etic category but straddled both the etic and emic. After saying that her mother looked like she was a "villager," Wafa exclaimed, "Shee ma byenhamal," which literally means "something that cannot be carried"—"unbearable." The incident made me start to register far more methodically the way my informants deployed a Newtonian physics-like imaginary to speak of their state of being.

The notion of field, then, as I hope I have shown, offers us—in the way it allows the physical, the social, and the existential to intermingle, coalesce, and fuse—the basis of a whole socioexistential physics of our life struggles. In learning habitus and capital, students are often invited to think of Bourdieu's conception of the social as an ocean. When we know how to swim, our bodily strength, our style, and our technical prowess affect our capacity to move in such an environment. In highlighting the active forces that constitute the field, however, Bourdieu is also inviting us to think of the ocean as oceans are: full of waves, currents, swells, rips—that is, forces that move us in all kinds of directions. What we are carrying, whether it slows us down or propels us, matters. But, just as important, what also matters is our relation to those currents and forces, how well we can read them, and how well we can harness them to our advantage: Do we know how to move with rather than resist a current? Or how to catch a wave? It our relation to the social forces surrounding us that determines in what way and to what extent they shape our socio-existential mobility.

Conclusion: Viability and the Politics of Existential Ecologies

In this book I have gone through Pierre Bourdieu's key categories, highlighting the way they help us delineate, first, a conception of the social as an economy concerned with the production and distribution of being and, second, a conception of social agents propelled by the desire to augment their being, or what I have also referred to as their social viability. To recapitulate: In habitus we located Bourdieu's interest in the relation between viability and the degree of efficiency with which the human mind-body assemblage deploys itself in the world—how well it is able to categorize the world and how well it can act in it. There is in habitus, I argued, a vitalist conception that is continuously in dialogue with a whole tradition that sees the viability of life as capacity to act, as energy, power, efficiency, and force. *Illusio*, on the other hand, offers us a very different conception of being and viability, having to do with the existence of a raison d'être. As I have argued, *illusio* points to an existential form of viability whereby a viable life is a life structured around fulfilling pursuits that make the existence of the social agents and their surroundings meaningful and worthwhile. Capital—and particularly, as I noted, symbolic capital—proposes a third dimension of social viability associated with degrees of recognition. Here Bourdieu inherits a largely Hegelian set of questions related to *recognition* and transforms them into a political economy that involves the inheritance, distribution, and augmentation of the legitimacy and valorization of one's achievements, one's lifestyle, one's pursuits, and so on. Last but not least, I have argued that the concept of field, far from just denoting a space where all these versions of being and viability are played out, adds a further dimension which relates this being and viability to experiences of socioexistential mobility.

But, as the notion of struggle in the conception of fields brings to the fore, Bourdieu's conception of the social world is not merely that of an economy of being but of a *political* economy of being. *Political* means, first, that the production, distribution, and pursuit of social viability is structured by relations of power and domination and as such is rife with inequalities and injustices. Second, *political* means people are never left alone to augment their social viability as they please. Being efficient, having a meaningful pursuit, and being recognized involve a continuous struggle against those who aim to monopolize the resources necessary to conduct a viable life and who try to impose their own conceptions of what that life entails. People do not just passively inherit the social viability that the social world has distributed and put before them. While they do come into a position from the day they are born, such as a class location, and find themselves on a class trajectory, they nonetheless struggle to position themselves as best as they can from that position. And though they inherit a certain amount of capital, they also struggle to augment it, compete for its distribution, and struggle to valorize it. In so doing, social agents are not only continuously struggling to do as best as they can with the world that they have inherited but are also continuously involved in actively making the social world conducive to their augmentation of being—to keep social reality on their side, as it were. They are incessantly engaged in making and unmaking reality, which is what Bourdieu defines as the main feature of politics.[1] Viability-seeking social agents are political to the extent that they strive to transform the world into the ecological environment that best suits their modes of existence, which includes their definitions, practices, and pursuits of the viable life.

It is in this sense that this dimension of the political can be conceived as a struggle for the construction and institution of existential ecologies. To fully understand what this entails we need to further examine the ontological nature of Bourdieu's social constructivism.

Symbolic Power and Existential Ecologies

In our examination of the notions of habitus, *illusio*, and capital in the previous chapters, it was made clear that these concepts help us depict the way people both struggle to fit into the world and struggle to shape the world in such a way that it suits them. Each of these categories depicts modes of construction of a surrounding that is most suitable for one's existence. The practices that emanate from a habitus shape the social world practically: They sculpt it, mold it, and carve it such that it is well suited to the deployment of the self. Habitus has a conatus at its core. As I have argued, it involves a continuous struggle of adjusting to the world and also of giving shape to the world so it is adjusted to us. In this sense, practices construct the world in the way hikers forge a path in the forest, sometimes following the path already traced by others before them or sometimes feeling impelled to create a new one. The more people go along the path, the more salient and well-traced the path becomes. The habitus of a collectivity can be imagined to be constructing the lived world in a similar fashion: tracing the paths that can be trodden and even establishing how they can be trodden.

The investment in social reality that is presupposed by *illusio* also involves a construction of the real, albeit in an entirely different way. Being a principle of meaningfulness, *illusio* is a differentiator between the important and the unimportant, the significant and the insignificant, the meaningful and the meaningless, always as a matter of degree rather than in an either/or fashion. Here construction is done through a process of selecting, highlighting, and intensifying the presence of those aspects of reality that are important, significant, or meaningful to our pursuit and, by the same token, pushing back, effacing, and making recede those other elements that are not important or are less so.

Finally, the dimensions of social being highlighted by capital also have a specific mode of world-making associated to them. The social construction of the world occurs via processes of recognition and legitimation: The more collective recognition and legitimacy a social reality is accorded, the more real it is. Here again, as we have seen in so many other instances, Bourdieu's economic logic of differentiation prevails: Things are not either real or not real, but are more or less real. And what characterizes the dominant cultural forms is their capacity to assert themselves and be experienced as more real than others. An individual cultural practice has less social reality than a collectively shared cultural practice. A shared *illusio* that has become, as Bourdieu calls it, a *collusio* turns into a collective aspiration that is materially present in the very constitution of the social world. We can understand this distinction by picturing a society where gambling is perceived as an individual, nonsanctioned *illusio* and where its presence is limited to a few small illegal gambling joints. In contrast to such a society, we can imagine one that collectively sanctions and valorizes gambling. The latter will be dotted with bars filled with poker gaming machines, and big casinos will dominate the cityscape.

All the above ultimately entails for Bourdieu that social agents are continuously engaged in a symbolic struggle to institute reality. It is important to be as clear as possible regarding what Bourdieu means by "institute" and by "symbolic." We can begin by noting that, in the French sociological tradition and in French language generally, the verb *instituer* has a meaning that is not present in the English verb *to institute* or in the terminology associated with the word *institution*.[2] In French it means to establish and create a state of affairs in a durable manner. As such, to institute a practice is to stabilize it and make it something durable and more socially salient rather than fleeting. This is regardless of whether it becomes integrated into an *institution*, as we understand that term. Society is, by definition, a largely "instituted" reality. That is what differentiates a societal reality from a passing event or a fleeting process. Institutions, especially the state, clearly play an important role in the establishment of this salience and durability. But more than institutions, it is a process of symbolic domination that is behind all social realities with a semblance of stability and durability.

Regarding "symbolic," it is important to note that one doesn't understand much about the term if one takes Bourdieu's conception of the symbolic to mean something opposed to material. "Symbolic," for Bourdieu, is not conceived any differently from the way it is used by the structuralist tradition around Louis Althusser, Jacques Lacan, and Claude Lévi-Strauss. In that tradition, the symbolic is not something mental or ideational as opposed to "material" reality. The symbolic order is the order of symbolized reality—that is, meaningful reality. It is not symbol versus reality but "symbolized reality" versus raw reality, reality for us versus reality in itself. The latter is there but inaccessible to us other than in a symbolized form—what Lacan calls "the Real."[3]

That Bourdieu highlights the practical at the expense of the structural dimensions of social life affects how this symbolic order is approached, but not its general ontological nature. As I have already noted, the reason why the struggle over the valorization of capital is at the heart of symbolic politics is that it entails a struggle over the means of classification, perception, and appreciation of what constitutes a meaningful and treasured life pursuit. What needs to be highlighted here is that this struggle is nothing more or less than the struggle to ensure that social reality is "on your side," as it were: that it speaks the language that you speak, that it valorizes what you valorize, and that it considers important and shines a light on what you deem worthy of considering important and shining a light on. That is why Bourdieu sees in symbolic power the power to make and unmake reality. In this sense, symbolic domination secures a general dimension of viability. One might even call it a meta-viability in that it is the precondition of all the forms of viability related to habitus, *illusio*, and capital. When you look at the concept of efficiency pertaining to habitus, for instance, a body cannot be efficient or inefficient in the abstract. A body is efficient or inefficient *in* a particular material environment, a particular reality. Consequently, the struggle for efficiency is always a reality struggle at the same time as it is a struggle to make the body more capable and most suited for that reality. This is why all struggles are reality struggles, struggles for a viability derived from the degree to which social agents have a relation of *complicity* with social reality (i.e., the degree to which social agents and social reality are well suited for each other and partake in each other's struggles).

Symbolic power highlights another anthropological dimension that is present in Bourdieu's work: the idea that we humans are ecological beings. We are ecological beings in the sense that, through our existence, we create the very ecology/environment in which we exist and that ends up affecting how we exist. Other philosophers and social scientists have used different terms to refer to this ecology: *social environment*, *lifeworld*, *experiential reality*, *discursive reality*, and the like. All these concepts point to the circular idea (which is circular in a good way) that as we come to exist in the world, we largely inherit a world that has been made into "our world" by those who bequeathed it to us and, likewise, we continue to strive to shape the world into a world that suits us best, where we can best strive. This is an individual and a collective power.

Ideally, and idealistically, everyone, by the mere fact of being practically enmeshed in the world, has the power to shape their own reality as they see fit. But, of course, this is never the case. We are born in a world that is already built by those who preceded us. And as I have already noted, we are born in a specific location within this world and on a specific trajectory. For Bourdieu, a social location and a social trajectory are specific relations to the world. Thus, we inherit the world in ways that are specific to our location and trajectory. In the process, depending on our relation to those who have built the world in which we come to exist, we inherit degrees of complicity with the world. Likewise, we are not left alone with our inheritance to build or reproduce the world as we see fit. The dominant groups have more power than others to shape the reality in which they exist. It is a characteristic of their dominance. As such, they end up subjecting the dominated to the realities that are best suited to the dominant. The dominated struggle to fit into a world that is not made by or for them, and where the degree of complicity they have with such a world is minimal. It is through this ontological imposition that the dominants transform their symbolic power into symbolic domination.

Symbolic Domination as Ontological Domination

Symbolic power, then, is the power to create one's own ecological sur-rounding, the social reality where one thrives. Symbolic domination, by distinction, occurs when the dominant force their own social reality on others. In so doing, they make others strive to augment their being in a reality that is their own and that is always already rigged against them. This symbolic/ontological domination ensures that the dominant group's practices yield an augmented sense of being while the dominated end up with a diminished sense of being. That is, it ensures that the practices of the dominant are efficient and well-fitted to their environment, able to yield both existential meaningfulness and recognition from others. Dominated practices are the opposite. They are inefficient. They are meaningless in that engaging in them does not give one a sense that life is worth living. And they yield little recognition. They are sick practices—and I'm only partly using *sick* in a metaphoric manner here—because "sick" in French is *malade* (in English we have the connected word *malady*), and *malade*, as those who have studied the history of the usage of the term *habitus* tell us, is actually a contraction of *mal-habitus*. A person who is socially *malade* is someone who is socially "sick" in the sense of not being able to deploy themself well in the world.[4]

I have often struggled to find a good way of communicating this no-tion of a "real, constructed reality" to people who for a variety of reasons find it hard to imagine. And I'll allow myself to deploy here the same wild example that I have deployed many times while teaching only because, despite its unrealness, it has been thus far relatively effective in conveying what Bourdieu has in mind. So here we go.

Skis allow you to move better on snow according to how well you mas-ter them. Fins allow you to move much more easily in water according to how well you master them. In Bourdieu's world, there is a Darwinian, or perhaps more Lamarckian, process in which the body trying to move on snow eventually develops ski-like features while the body trying to move in water develops finlike features—bodily dispositions that allow one to operate maximally in one's environment. This is what, after Benedict de Spinoza's notion of "perfection," we have referred to as the maximal abil-ity to deploy oneself efficiently in the world. The "augmentation" of this perfection is what Spinoza says causes us to experience joy. I have already noted the influence of this Spinozan vitalism on Bourdieu's conception of practical efficacy. Furthermore, Bourdieu explicitly uses a Spinozan concept, conatus, to describe the core part of the habitus that always aims to reproduce itself in its being.

To go back to our example, in Bourdieu's world of skiing (the world of people with a skiing *illusio*), people are invested in skiing, develop a skiing habitus, and accumulate being by pushing themselves to master skiing in the best possible way by accumulating varieties of "skiing capital": strength, technique, grace, better equipment, and the like. Likewise, in the world of swimming (the world of the people with a swimming *illusio*), people are invested in swimming and they strive to accumulate "swimming capital." So far, so good, one might say, in that there is a very Spinozan struggle to seek joy happening through the accumulation of practical efficacy within the world of skiing, where the world is mainly snow, and within the world of swimming, where the surrounding world is mainly water. The difficulty in understanding Bourdieu's concept of politics is that it highlights another important dimension to this struggle—one that takes us away from the Spinoza-inspired accumulation of practical efficiency.

To understand Bourdieu here you have to imagine—and this is where I am asking the reader to stretch their imagination a bit—that the snow-filled reality of skiers and the water-filled reality of swimmers are not givens, like an unchanging environmental reality. Instead the bodies equipped with skis are also equipped with miniature personal snow-making machines. They are personally and collectively busy creating the very world in which they can operate best. Indeed, their snow-covered world will only exist insofar as they succeed in creating the snow on which they can maximize their movement.[5]

Likewise, with the bodies endowed with fins. They not only have fins but are also equipped with water-flooding devices trying to turn everything into a swimmable reality. It is here that we come to the struggle that is of interest to Bourdieu: While the struggle for the augmentation of being among skiers in the field of skiing and among swimmers in the field of swimming is important, the most far-reaching struggle is the one between snow-producing skiers and water-producing swimmers. Here the competition is not merely over who skis or swims better, over who respectively gets to define and accumulate skiing capital and swimming capital, but over whether the world itself is going to be a skiing world or a swimming world. Here the winner imposes both their reality and their practical mastery over reality. If the skiers win, we end up with a lot of people looking ridiculous, wearing swimsuits and fins and trying to walk in the snow. And if the swimmers win, we get the equally ridiculous situation of a bunch of people in full ski gear trying to cross the lake of life, as it were. This is what Bourdieu calls the struggle for "making and unmaking social worlds." I will stop here with this wild heuristic analogy as it is already beyond the pale to stretch it further. But, for what it's worth, the reader needs to also remember that, for Bourdieu, even if snow reality dominates, water reality will still have a minor existence to the extent that there remain people with a finlike habitus. There are dominant and dominated people within a reality; but just as—if not more—important, there are dominant and dominated realities. It is worth noting that despite the "classically French" intellectual animosity between them, and despite their real differences,[6] Bourdieu and Jacques Rancière share a similar affinity toward this ontologically oriented politics. In *Disagreement*, Rancière defines politics as being primarily "made up of relationships between worlds."[7] In *Dissensus*, he also argues that "the essence of politics is dissensus. Dissensus is not a confrontation between interests or opinions. It is the demonstration (manifestation) of a gap in the sensible itself. Political demonstration makes visible that which had no reason to be seen; it places one world in another."[8]

It is this conception of a struggle between opposing realities that constituted the basic framework Bourdieu used in his early work, even before he developed the notion of habitus, to understand and analyze the practical decision-making processes of the Algerian peasantry in the face of social change. He aimed to show that capitalism did not merely introduce new practices that the peasants were not capable of mastering. Rather, these practices forced on the peasants a new reality; the practices actually robbed them of the very reality in which they could operate, or at least made that reality a minor, dominated reality.[9] In *Travail et travailleurs en Algérie*, Bourdieu speaks of the Algerians' "confrontation with a situation in which no adequate action is possible." Using a term borrowed from the German neurologist and psychiatrist, Kurt Goldstein, he describes this as a "systematic functional disintegration."[10]

Modes of Domination

Bourdieu offers several key analytical concepts and differentiations that are concerned with elucidating the way power works in giving shape to the social world as a political economy of being rigged to favor the dominant groups. As is clear from his work, it is important to keep in mind that he approaches domination from three simultaneous perspectives. These are:

1   Domination as a relatively stable structure—that is, as an ongoing so-
    cial relation of subjection between dominant and dominated social
    groups with relatively stable and durable differential of accumulated
    capital and social power. Class relations, patriarchal relations, and
    colonial relations are all examples of this type of relation. This is the
    most "objectivist" of Bourdieu's conceptions of domination, in that
    these relations are perceived to exist for the social analyst even if those
    inhabiting the social are not aware of them.[11]

2   Domination as what the dominants do, as a practice, such as when we
    speak of "strategies of domination." But also, notably, what Bourdieu
    refers to as "the field of power," which treats "power" as the product
    of the accumulation of various forms of capital each competing to
    dominate the field of power itself. This is somewhat similar to what
    Karl Marx called "fractions of capital" in that it breaks the dominant
    into a variety of interests, all in a position of power, but all competing
    to dominate the field of power itself.[12]

3   Domination as a pervasive type and culture of power within the field.
    This entails a more totalizing analytic description of the existing state
    of domination instituted by the dominant class. It involves a further
    differentiation between

    A   modes of domination, which offer a description of the manner in
        which domination is instituted; here Bourdieu mainly differenti-
        ates between aristocratic and democratic domination

    B   degrees of domination, which offer an analytics of the extent to
        which a dominant group has saturated the social with its own
        values and imposed its reality on others; this is where the concept
        of symbolic violence does its analytical work

Bourdieu shares the first two approaches to domination (as structure
and as practice), at least at a general level, with many other social scientists. It is the third conception that is truly distinctive in his work and that
needs further detailing.

Let us begin with the differentiation between *aristocratic* and *democratic* domination. In a way, the categories are self-explanatory. *Aristocratic
domination* involves the dominant group positing, as aristocracies do, that
its mode of being, the kind of cultural capital it has, and its tastes and

modes of appreciation are superior to those of the rest of the population. What's more, the group posits that its possession of "what it takes" to be part of the dominant group and to have access to the kind of being this entails is a natural inheritable part of the group's members (e.g., "in the blood"). The dominated group is also posited to have a mode of being that is specific to it and that it inherits. It just so happens that this mode of being is constructed as inferior to the mode of being of the dominant group. Bourdieu sees traditional masculine domination as a classical aristocratic form of domination.[13] It institutes a division between what males are, what they can do, and what they can aspire to and what females are, what they can do, and what they can aspire to. Most important, it naturalizes what it takes to be a male and what it takes to be a female and the kind of social being open to each. In the way that differences between the dominant's social being and the social being of the dominated are naturalized, as well as in the superiority of the one over the other, *aristocratic domination* institutes a form of apartheid. Indeed, South African apartheid in the past and today's Zionist Israel can be seen as instituting or as having instituted a form of aristocratic ethnoracial domination. What each group is and what it has access to is predetermined by birth. Aristocratic domination is dependent on the dominated knowing their place by seeing it as their natural place. It essentializes the difference between the dominant and the dominated by institutionalizing it within both the social body and the human body. Thus, it is not only a matter of belief that stops the dominated from wanting to aspire to the dominant's mode of being but rather a question of the social avenues for self-realization being objectively structured in such a way that the body of the dominated is not able to realistically aspire to do certain things. For example, I'm pretty short (in case you don't know me, you'll have to take my word for it: I'm pretty short), and so, as a short body, first at school in Lebanon and then, in later life, in Australia, I realistically never aspired to play basketball professionally for the Los Angeles Lakers or the Chicago Bulls. Because of where I am located and because of my evaluation of what my body can achieve in relation to the possibilities offered by my social milieu, being a professional basketball player on a famous American team has not been one of my imaginary aspirations. Or, to put it in Bourdieusian language, professional basketball was never laid out as an *illusio* before me: I played basketball in school and could see that I wouldn't even make it on my school team let alone on a famous international team. This is not where my body can go. That does not mean that I cannot fantasize, but that is a different question. What is important

Conclusion

is that the question of dominated aspirations is not simply a matter of belief, something that you subjectively stop yourself from aspiring to. It is more that your body and society are constituted in such a way, in themselves and vis-à-vis each other, that makes it impossible for you to aspire to certain things. We go back to what we highlighted earlier: For Bourdieu, domination is the domination of social reality and a decline in the sense of complicity with social reality. The very notion of "confidently aspiring to be *x*" involves a sense of complicity. Aristocratic domination deprives the dominated of that sense when it comes to aspiring for something that the dominant do. It makes the dominated stick to what they experience ontologically as their realistic lot, unless they think it viable to struggle to reshape reality. As I was growing up, I never felt that a struggle to reshape American basketball into a game that accommodates short people from Lebanon was likely to succeed, so I simply accepted that it wasn't for me.

Let us now move to *democratic domination*, which works rather differently, at least up to a point. The democratic mode of domination, when one thinks of it, is a far more perverse form of domination. But let's start with its basic form. Rather than instituting a neat aristocratic division between a dominant and a dominated mode of being, in the democratic mode of domination the dominant take the reality with which they are most complicit and proclaim it to be the only mode of being that everyone, the dominant and the dominated, ought to aspire to. Here, instead of dominating by saying, "This is what we dominant do, and this what you dominated do," the dominant say, "*Everyone* should be *x*." But *x* is something that the dominant are already adept at. Here is a brief, clichéd example to highlight the difference. Let's take the ways an upper-class English accent and a working-class accent are spoken. In an aristocratic mode of domination, the upper class will tend to normalize the belief that their accent is superior to the working-class accent, but they may also aim to instill the belief that each accent reflects a different type of intelligence specific to each class. What's more, this level of intelligence is seen as an inheritance (in the blood). There is no point in the working class trying to speak any differently. The difference in accent becomes articulated to the difference in intelligence that, in turn, is articulated to class difference. In the democratic mode of domination, the ruling class will act differently. Its members will take its accent, and instead of positing it as their exclusive property by nature, they posit it as the "proper" accent that everyone should speak. Thus, rather than closing access to its accent, as the aristocrats do, it opens it up, and says to the working class, "Come on, you can do it, go ahead and try to speak 'proper' English." The problem is that those from the ruling class have already learned to speak with that accent from the day they were born. It is their mother tongue, what they inherit and deploy in their households. It is integral to their way of life.[14] Their accent not only comes to them "naturally" but also has a relation of complicity to all aspects of their existence. That is, the accent is not a series of detached sound bites. It comes with the whole social reality to which it is articulated. The working classes try to speak it, but in so doing they can only try, as they are always trying to bridge not merely a linguistic gap but an ontological gap that exists between them and the reality to which the accent is articulated. As such, they find themselves in the position of those who are forever trying.

On the basis of this discussion, we can say that the aristocratic mode of domination institutes a structural relation of power between those who have x and those who have y, with x being posited as superior to y, while the democratic mode of domination institutes a structural relation between those who have x and those who are forever trying to have x without ever fully succeeding, with x being posited as the only mode of being worth pursuing. The aristocratic mode of domination works by instilling in the dominated a sense of inferiority and resignation that their lives can never be as viable as that of the dominant classes. The democratic mode of domination works by instilling in the dominated a sense of *failure*, a belief that it is because they lack something (energy, knowledge, intelligence, etc.) that they are not managing to access the kind of being the dominant classes have, even though it is there, on offer, for them to take. Although the capitalist class is seen as superseding the feudal class in the history of British capitalism, it can be said that early capitalism involved an aristocratic mode of class domination: working-class people, such as the exemplary miners, did not aspire to be part of the ruling class. They resisted by valorizing their own culture for what it was. In late capitalism, the rule of the capitalist class becomes more democratic. As the working classes gradually lose any sense of cultural specificity and pride in their "working-class culture," they increasingly become part of a generalized "popular" culture in which everyone is trying to join the middle class.

Note that the example above highlights an important point: Modes of domination in real life are neither aristocratic nor democratic; they are often a fusion or continual oscillation between both. Colonial racism has instituted white dominance by continually fluctuating between a belief that white people are essentially superior to Indigenous people—that nothing much can be done to help the latter, who aren't even human—and a belief that the natives can be saved if they are willing to ditch their modes of being and adopt the "evidently" superior white colonial mode of being. Furthermore, the dominant groups instituting a democratic mode of domination often resort to aristocratic strategies to keep the dominated in place. Take, for instance, the republican politics of assimilation in France. Here we have a classical process of instituting a democratic mode of domination. White French people insist that the republic is color- and ethnicity-blind and that anyone, regardless of their particularities, can become French if they accept and assimilate to the French secular republican spirit. Yet—and despite the game being rigged against those who wish to assimilate—when people take their assimilation too seriously and appear close to achieving it, the dominant worry and start to produce or facilitate nativist (i.e., aristocratic) arguments that put the dominated in their place and inform them that one can only become a "really true" French person (*de souche*) if one is white. This dynamic is highlighted in the case of France because of the strong (mis) belief in the color-blindness of the republican ideal. But the dynamic is present in all colonial and settler-colonial states. As I have shown in my book *White Nation*, it also pervades the politics of belonging in multicultural Australia.[15] It is also the key feature of the politics of "assimilation" toward Indigenous Australians. The politics of assimilation, in fact, offers a paradigmatic example of the process of symbolic violence. So I will use it as a point of entry into the concept to explain two key questions: Why "symbolic"? Why "violence"?

"Assimilation" in Australia emerged in the early to mid-twentieth century as an ideology and as a politics that posits itself as nonracist when compared to the belief that Indigenous Australians are a lower kind of humanity destined to disappear. This is because inherent to the assimilationist ideology is the presupposition that Indigenous people can indeed become like white people. There is no radical racial separation between them that forbids this, as "the racists," who believe in an insurmountable gap between Black and white people, proclaim. What we have then is a classical opposition between an aristocratic and a democratic form of domination. But, as described above, the victory of assimilationism did not mean that Indigenous Australians did indeed assimilate. It meant that those who were captured by it as an instituted reality were caught in a space where they were always destined to be categorized as "failures"—Indigenous bodies that are "sick," in the sense described above, forever trying to assimilate but never really managing to do so.

Conclusion

This is where the "violence" of symbolic domination begins. Assimilation as a mode of symbolic violence not only generates sick bodies that cannot deploy themselves in the world as they are expected to. Worse still, it generates bodies that despite their "sickness" continue to believe in their capacity to achieve what they cannot achieve, as it is all they have available to them to believe in.

Imagine me, in the example I gave above about the relation between my short body and the world of professional basketball and its tall bodies. What if instead of realistically coming to terms with the fact that the world of professional basketball is not for me, my school and later experience led me to believe that in fact this is what I should aim for in life? My life would have consisted of a frustrating, physically and psychologically debilitating history of continual belief in something I cannot achieve: an ongoing repetitive series of failed attempts at trying to give my life a meaning and a sense of purpose. This is why, as I noted above, the history of assimilation is a good exemplification of the kind of violence that is symbolic violence. It is a symbolic violence that truly batters the body as it makes it continually desire that which will defeat it. I am sure that had Lauren Berlant had a better knowledge of Bourdieu's work, they would have seen in his conception of symbolic violence a very particular but very intense conception of "cruel optimism."[16] The latter is indeed a perverse mode of diminishing one's being while thinking that it is all up to you to try and, if you succeed, the augmentation of your being is just around the corner.

Colonialism constitutes perhaps the clearest and most paradigmatic example of this ontologically conceived symbolic domination that ensures and reproduces the sickness of the dominated. When the Europeans invaded the Americas, they did not merely "dominate" the Indigenous people who inhabited them. They transformed the whole social and existential ecology of the continent. They forced their world, their lifestyle, their aspirations, and their life pursuits onto the continent and instituted them. They not only robbed the Indigenous people of their freedom, exploited them, and exploited their resources but also robbed them of their whole social reality and repositioned them in an implanted European social reality within which they were ill-equipped to augment their being. This is why, as we have noted, the concept of symbolic violence begins to take shape in Bourdieu's work in his analysis of the way the Algerian peasants experienced the implantation of French colonialism on their lands. The peasants were not oppressed within French capitalist society in the way the French working class were said to be oppressed by capital within a French society that they shared with the dominant capitalist exploiting class. The peasants, as colonized people, were outside this society and dominated by its totality. Both the French capitalists and the French workers who shared this totality were party to this ontological domination.

At the most basic level, then, symbolic violence is a particularly deep, intense, and pervasive imposition of the reality of the dominant on the dominated. What makes such an imposition so complete is that it stops being seen as an imposition. Instead of it being experienced as the reality of the dominant, it becomes experienced as "reality" tout court. Bourdieu refers to this as a naturalization of domination—that is, something that dominates no longer carries the trace of its domination and becomes perceived as "natural." Along with this comes the work of "fatalization"—That is, making the future something unchanging that one cannot do much to alter, a fatality. This, at the same time, gives the dominant a "predictive" power. As Bourdieu puts it in one of his lectures, "This power of prediction, prophetic, of fatalization is symbolic power par excellence."[17] This is why he sees the main object of a social science that tries to undo symbolic violence as being a work of denaturalization and defatalization.[18]

A quick example of naturalization can be helpful here. In all parts of the Western world, if you ask someone what date it is, they will have no problem replying quickly and unambivalently. Let's say it is December 7. The reply comes: "It's the seventh of December." Usually, the reply is unqualified. There is no "I think it is . . ." or "To me, it is . . ." It comes as a conveyance of an incontrovertible, indisputable, and boring fact. On the day when the calendar tells us it is December 7, "seventh of December" seems like a *natural* date to most of us—natural in the sense of "This is how it is." But had they been a historian of the way the Western world has come to categorize and classify time, the person who answered this question might have said, "Actually, there is a long history of struggle between the Gregorian calendar and the non-Gregorian calendar, and the fact that today is the seventh of December is due to the fact that we have naturalized the dominance of the Gregorian calendar." The Gregorian calendar has lost the history of its dominance.[19] This is the idea of symbolic violence: symbolic violence is when we naturalize the reality within which we are living, when we naturalize its categories and the aspirations that emerge from it. *Naturalize*, here, derives its meaning from a somewhat old-fashioned understanding of the nature/culture opposition, whereby the cultural is human-made and the natural is not. To naturalize something is to see it in the same way one sees a natural phenomenon. It is what it is, not because humans made it this way but because that is how it is. Once we do this we start thinking of social reality as unalterable or at least as far more resistant to social change than if we perceive it as a human construction.

Bourdieu differentiates states of symbolic violence from states of orthodoxy. States of orthodoxy are states where the domination of the dominants is secure but is visible for what it is. The dominated look at them and say, "They are ruling over us" or "They are forcing their interests and/or values on us." In a state of orthodoxy, the dominated perceive the dominance of the ruling group but are either ideologically or with brute force made to accept it, even though they are aware that the ruling group's interest is not their interest. In a state of orthodoxy, the ruling group has to labor to maintain its rule and dominance. In a state of symbolic violence, its dominance self-reproduces. "The dominant are drawn toward silence," Bourdieu argues, and symbolic violence is a silent mode of domination in that, once it is achieved, the ruling classes do not need to speak to justify it. To make noise to justify "self-evident principles which go without saying and would go better unsaid" is to already undermine their "go without saying" status.[20] Symbolic violence is a fantasy of maximal domination. In a state of symbolic violence, the dominated experience the aspirations and interests of the ruling group as their own, even if they rarely ever get to a situation where they feel they have obtained what they have aspired for. Here the dominated live in a reality that has successfully immunized itself from the historical process that has led to their domination.

Ideally, and perhaps idealistically, a struggle for domination between two groups can be seen as starting as a fight between equals, where the gaze of each competitor on the other is horizontal. It's like tennis, boxing, football, or any game involving two sides facing each other. To say that the gaze of the players/fighters is horizontal is to say that each side has equal power and is struggling from the same level with a kind of "you or we will prevail in this game." There is no a priori dominant or winner. But in social reality, hardly any "game of life" is played in this way, for the rules of the game and its reality are always on somebody's side more than the other. The dominated find themselves fighting the dominant, and the fact is that the rules are such that the game is always a priori rigged in the dominants' interest. That is, the way the game is instituted and played is already in a state of complicity with the dominant's mode of playing. As Bourdieu puts it: "Without being, strictly speaking, rigged, the competition resembles a handicap race that has lasted for generations or games in which each player has the positive or negative score of all those who have preceded him, that is, the cumulated scores of all his ancestors."[21]

As the foregoing discussion highlights, in conceiving politics as the politics of making and unmaking reality, Bourdieu argues that every domination involves both a struggle to dominate and an attempt to institute and, better still, *institutionalize* one's domination.[22] And this is where an important transformation occurs: the more the dominant institutionalize their dominance, enshrine it in law and by habit, among other things, the more their struggle moves from merely winning against someone to ensuring that the game and its rules are their game and their rules. Here, their gaze turns into a top-down gaze rather than just a horizontal gaze. From an imaginary of war, where the horizontal "I'm fighting you in this game" gaze prevails, we move to an imaginary of policing, where the top-down "I am protecting the whole game" gaze is dominant. Symbolic violence occurs at the most intense point of the process whereby the dominant, rather than being seen as fighting for their interests, become seen as—and indeed in practice become—the protectors of "the order of things." This is where the group that the dominant are struggling to subdue becomes a policing problem rather than a competitor/adversary.

A shift between warring and policing is very crucial in the fluctuation between states of orthodoxy and states of symbolic violence. We can briefly take the difference in the international politics of Donald Trump's Republican Party and Joe Biden and Kamala Harris's Democratic Party. The period following World War II was the apex of a belief in the United States not as a state pursuing its own interest alone but as a protector of an international order marked by democracy and the rule of law. It can be said that during that time, the dominance of US interest approximated a state of symbolic violence. But this international legitimacy has been in decline ever since. It can be said that US dominance in world politics has been more and more recognized for what it is: the United States fighting to realize its own interests under the guise of protecting a "world order of things."

What is interesting about Trumpian international politics is that it involves accepting this state of affairs and dropping any pretense of being responsible for policing the world order. It involves abandoning the American commitment to international bodies that provide a semblance of world governmentality and the United States unequivocally presents itself as fighting for its own national interests before anything else. The Trumpian Republican gaze on international politics can be said to be more horizontal than top-down. It looks at international competitors eye to eye and says, "I am going to win against you." In this, it can be seen as far more of a realist about the state of US domination and legitimacy than the Biden/Harris Democratic Party. The latter still has a fantasy of symbolic violence as it struggles to portray US international politics in terms of an international order that it sees itself as caring for and policing though it finds itself increasingly unable to do so.

More generally today, one can say that symbolic violence is an increasingly impossible fantasy of power. This is in the sense that while there's still an aspiration for symbolic violence everywhere, there are very few spaces where power and domination are so extremely naturalized that they constitute a case of symbolic violence such that we are dominated by them without seeing them as domination. In fact, we can say that we live in the era of the decline of symbolic violence. This is an era in which many of the key beliefs, values, and aspirations that were constitutive of capitalist modernity—such as development, progress, the superiority of the West, and human dominion over nature—are no longer naturalized. The same goes for white racial supremacy and masculine domination. Today we increasingly question these categories of domination and see them for what they are. Even categories that we once considered natural, such as the nation-state, are coming undone.

When I was growing up in the 1960s, the idea that France could witness separatist tendencies or that Scotland might secede from the United Kingdom was unthinkable, at least to us living outside those spaces. Today the fragility and possible disintegration of nation-states is taken for granted. This is not to say that masculine domination or developmental/domesticating modes of interacting with nature no longer exist or that nation-states are not dominant as a normative mode of collective being. Of course they are dominant. But they are explicitly recognized as dominant and they are increasingly challenged. From being part of a state of symbolic violence they have become orthodoxies.

One could move from this observation to say that symbolic violence is no longer useful to account for the way the main forms of domination work today. This, however, would fail to appreciate the depth at which symbolic violence operates and marks everyday life. For Bourdieu, symbolic violence is not only about the content of beliefs and the nature of reality. It reaches down into the very categories we have at our disposal for thinking about reality and our current situation. This is a common Bourdieusian theme: How does one think about domination when the categories with which we must think about it are themselves the product of this domination? Thus, in his analysis of the state, Bourdieu's primary question was something like, "How can I analyze the state, when the language and concepts I have at my disposal have been inculcated in me by the state?"[23] This question is very similar to the decolonial question posed today by so many: How can one think against colonialism when one's categories of thinking are deeply shaped by colonialism? The same applies for any situation of symbolic violence, and to fully understand the question's ramification, we need to clarify one last concept that Bourdieu considers crucial in his political economy of being. This is the concept of social reflexivity.

Being, Reflexivity, and Lucidity

It is often the case that people explaining and critiquing Bourdieu's concept of social reflexivity take it to be something that sociologists do.[24] Bourdieu himself often contributes to this understanding. Nonetheless, in his seminars at the École des Hautes Etudes en Sciences Sociales, some of which I attended, Bourdieu dealt with what he called the "social conditions of lucidity." I don't believe these seminars have been published, but I am sure some notes must be left in the archives. In any case, the reason I am referring to them is because in those lectures the capacity for lucidity is very much linked to the capacity for social reflexivity—the capacity to reflect on the social conditions that mark what you are and what you do. In other places Bourdieu has reflected on the degree of lucidity of the people he interviews and tries to explain why some interviewees are more able to make clear the conditions of their own making than others.[25] In these cases, lucidity involves social reflexivity, the ability to think through one's social location, one's inheritances, one's perspective, and the various social determinations that help make the reality one is enmeshed in what it is. This includes the inheritance or acquisition of an ability to distance oneself and "reflect" on one's existence. From a sociological perspective, this capacity, for Bourdieu, is not a matter of intelligence but of social location. For example, it can come as a result of being inserted in several realities that allow one a comparative lucidity. It can also come from being located in multiple contradictory social locations at the same time. What is clear is that social reflexivity is not only what sociologists do, since everyone engages in some form or another of it. But, like everything else for Bourdieu, the capacity for social reflexivity is not equally distributed in and by society. Social scientists work on making social reflexivity more professional, rigorous, and systematic: something that can be inherited as part of the sociological craft, but also something that can be conveyed to others.

The questions "Why do lucidity and social reflexivity matter?" and "Why do social scientists need to convey lucidity to others that are not, because of their social location, as able to engage in social reflexivity?" take us to the relations among social reflexivity, viability, and the political economy of being. For Bourdieu, social reflexivity allows us to augment our being by helping us acquire something priceless. It provides us with what he calls "a margin of freedom." As I have noted, Bourdieu is often seen—and, indeed, sees himself—as offering a deterministic critique of Jean-Paul Sartre's conception of the free subject who takes responsibility for their actions insofar as their actions begin with them and them only. For Bourdieu, this idea of a subject that is the starting point of practice and who is responsible for whatever action emanates from themself is a fiction. It flies in the face of the way so many of us are socially determined. For him, everything about us is socially determined, including the capacity of not being determined. Freedom from determination is not an anthropological given in the way Sartre imagines it. Rather, it is something that people wrest from the jaws of determination. The power to do so varies, and one of the key variables is people's capacity for social reflexivity and their ability to be lucid about their determinations. Bourdieu increasingly referred to the exercise of this ability as "socioanalysis."[26] It is the latter that opens up this precious social good called "a margin of freedom": the space where people can experience a liberty from determination, a liberty from domination and the possibility of other ways of augmenting their being.

Social scientists who by virtue of their social positioning and training can be virtuosos of socioanalysis are able to participate in this politics: the politics of undoing symbolic domination and creating "margins of freedom" where people can think through and develop more viable lives. But to do so, as Bourdieu insisted in *The Weight of the World*,[27] social scientists have to listen, understand, and help develop what emerges as a possibility in the social spaces and among the people they are analyzing. Implicit in the emphasis on "among the people they are analyzing" is the specter of its scholastic opposite, "among themselves and within academic culture." For the scholastically induced fantasy of creating liberatory spaces in the academic field as a substitute to, rather than as an integral part of, liberatory spaces elsewhere remains one of the key directions that politically inclined social analysts can easily head toward, and that an academic reflexivity and lucidity, a socioanalysis of the public intellectual posture, should help them avoid.

Notes

Preface

1 For a thorough and excellent investigation of Bourdieu's relation to colonial culture, see Pérez, *Bourdieu and Sayad Against Empire*.

Introduction

1 Bourdieu and Wacquant, *An Invitation to Reflexive Sociology*, 115. For such an interpretation of Bourdieu, see, for example, Lamont, *Money, Morals, and Manners*, 185: "Bourdieu shares with rational choice theorists the view that social actors are by definition socio-economic maximisers who participate in the world of economic exchange in which they act strategically to maximize material and symbolic payoffs."

2 Bourdieu, "Concluding Remarks," 274.

3 Spinoza, *Ethics*, 4, "Axiom," 2/241(P41, Dem), in *Collected Works*, 570.

4 Spinoza, *Ethics*, 3, "Definition of the Affects," 2/190, in *Collected Works*, 531–32.

5 Dreyfus and Rabinow, "Can There Be a Science of Existential Structure and Social Meaning?," 35.

6 Bourdieu, *Pascalian Meditations*. For an interpretation of Bourdieu sympathetic to this dimension, see Threadgold, *Bourdieu and Affect*, 30.

7 Bourdieu, *Travail et travailleurs en Algérie*, 11.

8 Bourdieu, *In Other Words*, 196.

9 Bourdieu, *Language and Symbolic Power*.

10 Bourdieu, *Pascalian Meditations*, 241.

11 Bourdieu, *Distinction*, 478; Bourdieu, "La dernière instance," 269; Bourdieu, *Practical Reason*, 52; Bourdieu, *The Social Structures of the Economy*, 218; Bourdieu, "Symbolic Capital and Social Classes," 296.

12 Hage, *The Racial Politics of Australian Multiculturalism*; Hage, "Bearable Life."

13 In a private chat Bourdieu once said to me something that stayed with me and that I later scribbled on a piece of paper. He said (not word for word): "I suppose it might be useful to start researching a space by thinking of some binary oppositions that one, as a researcher, thinks are crisscrossing it, as long as one then works to show why they are neither as binary nor as oppositional as they first seem, which, mind you, doesn't mean they are not there."

14 Hage, *The Racial Politics of Australian Multiculturalism*, 67.

15 As Nadler, *Think Least of Death*, 68, points out: "A free person, then, does not know gluttony, drunkenness, lust, greed, or ambition. Spinoza defines these vices as 'an immoderate love or desire for eating, drinking, sexual union, wealth and esteem.' As forms of love, they are directed at things that bring joy or pleasure. Ultimately, however, they result in sadness, as they all involve an eventual diminishing of one's overall *conatus* or power in body and mind."

16 Bourdieu, *Distinction*, 330.

17 Bourdieu et al., *La misère du monde*, 7. Please note that this is my own translation of this sentence, which differs from the one found in the English version of the book.

18 Heilbron, *French Sociology*.

19 Bourdieu, *Sketch for a Self-Analysis*, 41; Heilbron, *French Sociology*, 198; Pérez, *Bourdieu and Sayad Against Empire*, 55–56.

20 Bourdieu, *In Other Words*, 3–33.

21 See Shusterman, "Bourdieu as Philosopher."

22 Bolmain, *Pierre Bourdieu philosophe*; Braz, *Bourdieu*; Gautier, *La force du social*; Perreau, *Bourdieu et la phénoménologie*; "Pierre Bourdieu et la philosophie"; Meyer, "Présentation."

23 Lescourret, "Pierre Bourdieu," 26.

24 Bourdieu, *Distinction*, 472.

25 Dreyfus, *Being-in-the-World*, 6, claims that "Pierre Bourdieu says that in philosophy Heidegger was his 'first love.'"

26 As Bourdieu, "Scattered Remarks," 334, notes, "The conduct of genuine scientific research requires that one knows how to break oneself of all the habits of thought to which are attached the attributes of theoretical grandeur and depth: to abandon radical doubt in favor of a doubt proportionate to the degree of doubt in the thing, such as Leibniz recommended, to renounce the narcissistic satisfactions provided by all prestigious and sterile meta-discourses, whether methodological or epistemological, in favor of the methodically and epistemologically controlled production of new knowledge."

27 Bourdieu, *The Political Ontology of Martin Heidegger*; Bourdieu, *Outline of a Theory of Practice*, 73–76; Bourdieu, *Distinction*, 485–500.

28 Austin, *Sense and Sensibilia*, 3–4.

29 As Bourdieu, "The Scholastic Point of View," 381, notes, "Adoption of this scholastic point of view is the admission fee, the custom right tacitly demanded by all scholarly fields; the neutralizing disposition (in Husserl's sense) is, in particular, the condition of the academic exercise as a gratuitous game, as a mental experience that is an end in and of itself. I believe indeed that we should take Plato's reflections on *skholè* very seriously and even his famous expression, so often commented on, *spoudaios paizein*, 'to play seriously.'"

30 Bourdieu, "Intellectuals and the Internationalization of Ideas."

31 Bourdieu, *Pascalian Meditations*, 49.

32 Bourdieu, "The Philosophical Institution."

33 Nietzsche, *On the Genealogy of Morals*, 119.

34 Bourdieu, *General Sociology*, vol. 1, *Classification Struggles*, 127; Bourdieu, *Sociologie générale*, 1:187. This quote in the text is my translation of Bourdieu, "s'agissant du monde social, le perspectivisme tel que le définissait Nietzsche est indépassable," as it appears in Bourdieu, *Sociologie générale*. The passage is mistranslated in *Classification Struggles*: "as far as the social world is concerned, some degree of perspectivism as defined by Nietzsche is inevitable."

35 The tendency to see the scholastic approach to the world as bad social science is particularly present in Bourdieu's early critique of Lévi-Strauss's structuralism when he wanted to mark the specificity and originality of his theory of practice. But one can easily see, as I do, that his difference with Lévi-Strauss is a difference in their chosen research objects. See also Lentacker, *La science des institutions impures. Bourdieu critique de Lévi-Strauss.*

36 I have this particular formulation as a note taken during a class at the École des Hautes Etudes en Sciences Sociales. A student had made a remark about something (I no longer recall what), and Bourdieu replied, "C'est ce que j'appelle projeter notre relation particulière à l'objet dans l'objet." Bourdieu, in *The Logic of Practice*, 29, has noted the "projection of a nonobjectified theoretical relationship into the practice that one is trying to objectify," and Bourdieu and Wacquant, *An Invitation to Reflexive Sociology*, 68, notes "an uncontrolled relation to the object which results in the projection of this relation onto the object."

37 Bourdieu, *Pascalian Meditations*, 51; Bourdieu, *Retour sur la réflexivité*, 79.

38 Bourdieu, *The Logic of Practice*, 34.

39 Bourdieu, *Pascalian Meditations*, 9–10.

40 Bourdieu, *The Logic of Practice*, 34.

Chapter 1. Social Efficiency and Social Complicity

1 Emirbayer, "Tilly and Bourdieu," 411.

2 See, for example, Bidet, "Questions to Pierre Bourdieu."

3 Silva, "Unity and Fragmentation of the Habitus," 171; Swartz, *Culture and Power*, 101; Wacquant, "A Concise Genealogy and Anatomy of Habitus," 65.

4 Bourdieu, *Pascalian Meditations*, 138.

5 Bourdieu, *Outline of a Theory of Practice*, 72–78; Bourdieu, *The Rules of Art*, 179.

6 Bourdieu, *Sociologie générale*, 2:82.

7 Bourdieu, *The Logic of Practice*, 55.

8 Bourdieu, "Scattered Remarks," 340.

9 Bourdieu, "Men and Machines," 309.

10 Bourdieu, *The Logic of Practice*, 41.

11 Perreau, *Bourdieu et la phénoménologie*; Perreau, "Quelque chose comme un Sujet."

12 Lévi-Strauss assesses Bourdieu's criticism of him in much the same way. In response to Bourdieu's emphasis on strategies (as opposed to rules) of marriage, Lévi-Strauss, in Lévi-Strauss and Eribon, *Conversations with Claude Lévi-Strauss*, 103, asserts that "centers of interest shift over time. Sometimes the emphasis is on regulated aspects of social life, at others, on those elements where a certain spontaneity seems to occur. . . . It boils down to knowing what level of observation is the most profitable in the present state of knowledge and in light of a specific inquiry."

13 Connell, "The Black Box of Habit."

14 Tokarczuk, *Drive Your Plow over the Bones of the Dead*, 51–52.

15 Bourdieu and Wacquant, *An Invitation to Reflexive Sociology*, 140.

16 Bourdieu, *Sociologie Générale*, 2:1072–73, speaks of the specific power of those who have the capacity to "transform the practical, the confused, the vague that is of the essence of our experience of the social world into a discourse that is explicit, constituted, formalised, codified."

17 Bourdieu, *The Logic of Practice*, 55.

18 Bourdieu, "Men and Machines," indicates the kind of relationship operating here—"a quasi-ontological commitment flowing from prac-

tical experience" (306)—and suggests that this is in fact "what Heidegger, in his later works, and Merleau-Ponty (especially in *Le Visible et l'invisible*), endeavoured to express in the language of ontology, i.e. a 'savage' or 'barbarous'—I would say simply 'practical'—relationship to objects, falling short of intentionality" (316).

19 Bourdieu, "Algerian Landing," 419; Rey, "Faire le temps."

20 Heidegger, *Being and Time*.

21 Bourdieu, *Outline of a Theory of Practice*.

22 Bourdieu, *Pascalian Meditations*.

23 Bourdieu, *Outline of a Theory of Practice*.

24 Bourdieu, *Anthropologie économique*, 192.

25 Boas, "Anthropology"; see the discussion of Durkheim and Weber in Camic, "The Matter of Habit"; Tylor, *Primitive Culture*, 16.

26 Sparrow and Hutchinson, *A History of Habit*; Bennett, *Habit's Pathways*.

27 Bourdieu, "Forms of Capital," 241; Bourdieu, *Pascalian Meditations*, 215.

28 Pinto, "Pierre Bourdieu et la sociologie d'Émile Durkheim"; Wacquant, "Durkheim and Bourdieu."

29 Durkheim, *The Rules of Sociological Method*, 54.

30 Durkheim, "The Dualism of Human Nature," 44.

31 Malabou, *What Should We Do with Our Brain?*

32 Bourdieu and Wacquant, *An Invitation to Reflexive Sociology*, 122.

33 John Dewey, quoted in Bennett, *Habit's Pathways*, 165.

34 Halewood, "'Class Is Always a Matter of Morals,'" 386, emphasis in Dewey's original.

35 Merleau-Ponty, *Phenomenology of Perception*, 145–46.

36 Fanon, *Black Skin, White Masks*, 110.

37 Merleau-Ponty, *Phenomenology of Perception*, 144.

38 Wittgenstein, *Philosophical Investigations*, sec. 43.

39 As Mead, "Bourdieu and Conscious Deliberation," 66, puts it, "The world is made in this twin process of adjustment and construction, for the agent is always 'looking forward' to something, and is not simply facing a series of punctual presents."

40 Bourdieu, *Pascalian Meditations*, 162; Bourdieu, *The Logic of Practice*, 81.

41 Bourdieu, *Sociology in Question*, 177–80.

42 Bourdieu, *Outline of a Theory of Practice*, 233n15.

43 Bourdieu, "Outline of a Sociological Theory of Art Perception"; Bourdieu and Delsaut, "Pour un sociologie de la perception."

44 See Mead, "Forms of Knowledge."

45 Bourdieu, *The Logic of Practice*, 67.

46 Butler, *Excitable Speech*, 146.

47 James, *Habit*, 30.

48 Merleau-Ponty, *Phenomenology of Perception*, 145.

Chapter 2. Structure, Capacity, and Dispositionality

1 For an interesting discussion of this question, see Carlisle, *On Habit*.

2 Bourdieu, *Microcosmes*, 662.

3 Bourdieu, *Pascalian Meditations*, 215.

4 Bourdieu, "Structuralism and Theory of Sociological Knowledge," 705.

5 Bourdieu, *The Rules of Art*, 312.

6 Bourdieu, *Pascalian Meditations*, 141.

7 Bourdieu, *Outline of a Theory of Practice*, 72, 214n1.

8 See, for example, the authors deployed in Deleuze, *Difference and Repetition*, 5.

9 Héran, "La seconde nature de l'habitus," 388.

10 Héran, "La seconde nature de l'habitus," 403–8. See also, for example, Husserl, *Phenomenology and the Crisis of Philosophy*, 131.

11 See Bourdieu, *Political Interventions*.

12 Héran, "La seconde nature de l'habitus," 398; Husserl, *Zur Phänomenologie der Intersubjektivität*, 2:195.

13 Aristotle, *Metaphysics: Books Gamma, Delta, and Epsilon*, 1022b4; Plato, *Theaetetus and Sophist*, 197b10.

14 Rodrigo, "The Dynamic of *Hexis*," 10; Plato, *Theaetetus and Sophist*.

15 Rodrigo, "The Dynamic of *Hexis*," 11.

16 Bourdieu, *The Logic of Practice*, 59.

17 Steinmetz, "Social Fields, Subfields and Social Spaces," also notes the similarity between Bhaskar's critical realist categories and Bourdieu's. Bourdieu was also reported to note a resemblance between his approach and that of Bhaskar; see Vandenberghe, "'The Real Is Relational,'" 62.

18 Bhaskar, *A Realist Theory of Science*.

19 Bhaskar, *A Realist Theory of Science*, 190–219.

20 Héran, "La seconde nature de l'habitus," 388.

21 Aristotle, *Metaphysics: Book Theta*, 1046b29.

22 Bhaskar, *A Realist Theory of Science*, 7.

23 Bourdieu, *Sociologie générale*, 2:945.

24 Spinoza, *Ethics*, 3, "Postulates," 2/149, in *Collected Works*, 501.

25 Merleau-Ponty, *The Structure of Behavior*, 30.

26 James, "The Gospel of Relaxation," 133.

27 Husserl, *Ideas Pertaining to a Pure Phenomenology and to a Phenomenological Philosophy*, 2:195–98.

28 Hacking, "Science de la science," 162.

29 Bourdieu, *Pascalian Meditations*, 150.

30 Bourdieu, *The Logic of Practice*, 99–100.

31 Bourdieu, *Pascalian Meditations*, 138.

32 Bourdieu, *In Other Words*, 9.

33 Heidegger, "Building Dwelling Thinking."

34 Latour, *An Inquiry into Modes of Existence*; Viveiros de Castro, *Cannibal Metaphysics*.

35 Saussure, *Course in General Linguistics*, 140–41.

36 Lacan, *The Seminar of Jacques Lacan*, 3:63.

37 Kristeva, *Revolution in Poetic Language*.

38 As will be seen in chapter 3, one of Bourdieu's key terms, *sens*, indicates the depth of his commitment to directionality. As Dreyfus and Rabinow, "Can There Be a Science?," 38, note, "Bourdieu, like Merleau-Ponty, exploits the richness of the word *sens* to capture the directedness of comportment."

Chapter 3. On the Production and Distribution of the Meaningful Life

1 Cassin et al., "Sense/Meaning," 949; Rolland de Renéville, *Itinéraire du sens*, 175–76.

2 Bourdieu and Wacquant, *An Invitation to Reflexive Sociology*, 116.

3 Huizinga, *Homo Ludens*, 11.

4 Huizinga, *Homo Ludens*, 5.

5 Bourdieu, *Pascalian Meditations*, 207; Hacking, *The Emergence of Probability*, 94.

6 Bourdieu, *Pascalian Meditations*, 11.

7 Bourdieu, *The Rules of Art*, 33; Bourdieu, "Préface," 11; Bourdieu, *Pascalian Meditations*, 222.

8   As Sartre, *Existentialism Is a Humanism*, 29, writes, "Thus, we have neither behind us, nor before us, in the luminous realm of values, any means of justification or excuse. We are left alone and without excuse. That is what I mean when I say that man is condemned to be free: condemned, because he did not create himself, yet nonetheless free, because once cast into the world, he is responsible for everything he does."

9   Bourdieu, *Pascalian Meditations*, 239.

10 Bourdieu, *The Logic of Practice*, 66–67.

11 Bourdieu, *In Other Words*, 196.

12 Bourdieu, *Pascalian Meditations*, 240.

13 Bourdieu, *The Rules of Art*, 12–13.

14 Bourdieu, *Pascalian Meditations*, 140–41.

15 Bourdieu, *Pascalian Meditations*, 239.

16 Heidegger, "Building Dwelling Thinking," 374, 348, 349, 350.

17 Bourdieu, *Pascalian Meditations*, 240.

18 Pascal, *Pensées and Other Writings*, 45.

19 Chevallier and Chauviré, "Libido," in *Dictionnaire Bourdieu*, 99–100.

20 Bourdieu, *Pascalian Meditations*, 11.

21 Bourdieu, *Pascalian Meditations*, 164–68.

22 Bourdieu, *Distinction*, 86.

23 Freud, "Instincts and Their Vicissitudes," 121–22.

24 Jung, "Psychoanalysis and Neurosis," 247.

25 Bourdieu, *Pascalian Meditations*, 166; I have modified the translation, as "psychanalyse" is rendered as "psychology" rather than "psychoanalysis" in Richard Nice's English translation.

26 Bourdieu, "From Ruling Class to Field of Power," 35.

27 Bourdieu, *Pascalian Meditations*, 166.

28 Bourdieu, *Pascalian Meditations*, 151.

29 Bourdieu, *The Logic of Practice*, 66.

30 Bourdieu, *The Logic of Practice*.

31 Marx, *Capital*, 48–49.

32 Godelier, "System, Structure and Contradiction in Capital," 93.

33 Maître and Bourdieu, "Avant-propos dialogué," 9.

34 As Bourdieu, "The Philosophical Institution," 1, writes, "*Esse est inter-esse*: Being is being in, it is belonging and being possessed, in short,

participating, taking part, according importance, interest." See also Bourdieu, *On the State*, 272.

35 Bourdieu, in Bourdieu and Wacquant, *An Invitation to Reflexive Sociology*, 118, emphasis in the original.

36 Bourdieu, "The Contradictions of Inheritance," in Bourdieu et al., *The Weight of the World*, 512.

37 Bourdieu, *Pascalian Meditations*, 11.

38 Bourdieu, *The Logic of Practice*, 67.

39 Bourdieu, *The Logic of Practice*, 67.

40 Bourdieu, "The Philosophical Institution," 1.

41 Bourdieu, *Practical Reason*, 77.

42 Bourdieu, "Sociologists of Beliefs and Beliefs of Sociologists."

43 Bourdieu, *The Rules of Art*, 33.

44 Sartre, *Being and Nothingness*, 102–4.

45 Bourdieu, *The Rules of Art*, 12, 19; Bourdieu, "Annexe: Entretien de Pierre Bourdieu," 80.

46 Bourdieu, *The Rules of Art*, 12–13.

47 Bourdieu, *The Rules of Art*, 19, emphasis in the original.

48 Bourdieu, *The Rules of Art*, 13.

49 Bourdieu, *The Rules of Art*, 13.

50 Bourdieu, *Sociologie générale*, 2:668–69; Dubois, "Flaubert Analyste de Bourdieu."

51 Bourdieu, *The Rules of Art*, 9–20.

52 See Bourdieu, *The Social Structures of the Economy*; Bourdieu et al., *The Weight of the World*; and Bourdieu, *Travail et travailleurs en Algérie*.

53 Bourdieu, *The Field of Cultural Production*, 185–91.

54 Bourdieu, "The Invention of the Artist's Life," 87.

55 In Bourdieu and Chartier, "Gens à histoire, gens sans histoire," 57, Bourdieu defines social aging as a progressive closure from the world.

56 Bourdieu, "The Invention of the Artist's Life," 87.

57 Bourdieu, *Distinction*, 111.

58 Bourdieu and Saint Martin, *The State Nobility*, 45.

59 Bourdieu, *Distinction*, 110–11.

60 Hage, *The Diasporic Condition*, 43.

61 Hage, "Decay as Decline."

Chapter 4. The Means and Ends of Recognition

1   Calhoun, "Habitus, Field, and Capital," 69; Desan, "Bourdieu, Marx, and Capital," 332.

2   Bourdieu, "Forms of Capital," 243.

3   Bourdieu, "Les trois états du capital culturel."

4   Bourdieu, "Forms of Capital," 248–52.

5   Bourdieu, "Forms of Capital," 243.

6   Bourdieu, *Language and Symbolic Power*, 119, describes such a continuous distribution of masculinity, rendered discontinuous and categorical through public rites, which "[tend] to make the smallest, weakest, in short, the most effeminate man into a truly manly man, separated by a difference in nature and essence from the most masculine woman, the tallest, strongest woman, etc."

7   Hage, *The Racial Politics of Australian Multiculturalism*, 68–80.

8   Calhoun, "Habitus, Field, and Capital," 69.

9   Bourdieu, "Intellectual Field and Creative Project"; Bourdieu, *The Logic of Practice*, 112–13.

10 Bourdieu, "Condition de classe et position de classe," 212–13; Weber, *Economy and Society*, 932–33.

11 Bourdieu, *Sociology in Question*, 37.

12 Bourdieu, *The Social Structures of the Economy*, 5.

13 Mauss, *The Gift*, 100–102.

14 Bourdieu, *Distinction*, 375.

15 Bourdieu, *Distinction*, 246.

16 Bourdieu, "What Makes a Social Class?," 3–4, emphasis in the original.

17 Bourdieu, in Bourdieu and Wacquant, *An Invitation to Reflexive Sociology*, 98.

18 Bourdieu, "Forms of Capital," 241.

19 Bourdieu, "Forms of Capital," 248.

20 Bourdieu, "Les trois états du capital culturel," 3.

21 Bourdieu, in Bourdieu and Wacquant, *An Invitation to Reflexive Sociology*, 98, emphasis added.

22 Bourdieu, in Bourdieu and Wacquant, *An Invitation to Reflexive Sociology*, 101, emphasis in the original.

23 Pinto, *Pierre Bourdieu et la théorie du monde social*, 169.

24 Bourdieu, "What Makes a Social Class?," 3–4.

25 Foucault, *The Order of Things*, xvi.

26 Bourdieu, *Pascalian Meditations*, 242.

27 Bourdieu, "Social Space and Symbolic Power," 17.

28 Bourdieu, *Practical Reason*, 47.

29 Hegel, *Phenomenology of Spirit*, 110, para. 175; Bourdieu, "Scattered Remarks," 36. See also the anthropological account of recognition in Hegel provided in Kojève, *Introduction to the Reading of Hegel*.

30 Bourdieu, *Pascalian Meditations*, 241.

31 Bourdieu, *Pascalian Meditations*, 187.

32 Bourdieu, *Sociology in Question*, 135; Bourdieu and Delsaut, "Le couturier et sa griffe," 18.

33 I have to be honest and say that Bourdieu was not particularly enthralled when I suggested this relation and used it in my analysis of white modes of distinction in Hage, *The Racial Politics of Australian Multiculturalism*.

34 Freud, "The Sexual Theories of Children," 218.

35 Lacan, "The Signification of the Phallus."

36 Saussure, *Course in General Linguistics*, 138.

37 Freud, "The Sexual Theories of Children," 217.

38 For a discussion of the parallels between Bourdieu's concept of recognition and Lacan's description of the symbolic identification associated with the ego-ideal, see Steinmetz, "Bourdieu's Disavowal of Lacan," 453.

39 Bourdieu, "Social Space and Symbolic Power," 21.

40 Bourdieu, *Language and Symbolic Power*.

41 Bourdieu, *In Other Words*, 138.

42 Bourdieu, *Language and Symbolic Power*, 238.

43 Bourdieu, "Scattered Remarks," 336.

44 Bourdieu, *Pascalian Meditations*, 238, emphasis in the original.

Chapter 5. The Social Physics of Existential Mobility

1 Bourdieu, *Distinction*, 94.

2 For collections touching on various aspects of the concept, see Gorski, *Bourdieu and Historical Analysis*; and Hilgers and Mangez, *Bourdieu's Theory of Social Fields*.

3 Bourdieu, *In Other Words*, 88.

4 See, for example, Swartz, *Symbolic Power, Politics, and Intellectuals*, 75.

5 Bourdieu, *The Rules of Art*, 183.

6 As Bourdieu, *The State Nobility*, 386, puts it, "As autonomous fields multiply and the field of power diversifies, there is a move away from political indifferentiation and *mechanical solidarity* among interchangeable powers (such as clan elders or village leaders) or elementary forms of the division of the labor of domination into a small number of specialized functions (such as warriors and priests), away from simple systems dominated by one principle or the other, which include hierocracy and caesaropapism, and even the hereditary monarchy of divine right, systems doomed to open conflicts between temporal and spiritual authority" (emphasis in the original).

7 Mauss, *The Gift*, 100–102.

8 Bourdieu, *The Logic of Practice*, 117.

9 On the separation of church and state, see Bourdieu, *On the State*, 333. Regarding the economy, see Bourdieu, *The Social Structures of the Economy*, 6: "It was only very gradually that the sphere of commodity exchange separated itself out from the other fields of existence and its specific *nomos* asserted itself—the *nomos* expressed in the tautology 'business is business'; that economic transactions ceased to be conceived on the model of domestic exchanges, and hence as governed by social or family obligations ('there's no sentiment in business')" (emphasis in the original).

10 For the language he deploys in an early formulation of the field, see Bourdieu, "Structuralism and Theory of Sociological Knowledge," 690–91.

11 Bourdieu, *In Other Words*, 194.

12 Bourdieu, *In Other Words*, 88.

13 Bourdieu, *Pascalian Meditations*, 102.

14 Bourdieu, *Sociology in Question*, 73.

15 Bourdieu, *Sociology in Question*, 73–74.

16 Bourdieu, *Pascalian Meditations*, 112–13.

17 Bourdieu, *The Logic of Practice*, 68.

18 Bourdieu, *Microcosmes*, 662.

19 Bourdieu, *Practical Reason*, 32, emphasis in the original.

20 Bourdieu, *The Social Structures of the Economy*, 195, emphasis in the original.

21 Bourdieu, *In Other Words*, 192, emphasis in the original.

22 Bourdieu, *The Social Structures of the Economy*, 193.

23 Bourdieu, "What Makes a Social Class?," 3–4.

24 Bourdieu, *Distinction*, 94; Bachelard, *L'activité rationaliste*, 82.

25 Bourdieu, in Bourdieu and Wacquant, *An Invitation to Reflexive Sociology*, 100.

26 Bourdieu, *The Field of Cultural Production*, 148–50.

27 Bourdieu, in Bourdieu and Wacquant, *An Invitation to Reflexive Sociology*, 106, emphasis in the original.

28 Bourdieu, *Distinction*, 482.

29 Bourdieu, *Distinction*, 482–83.

30 See Beiser, *The German Historicist Tradition*, 346.

31 Bourdieu, *The Rules of Art*, 231.

32 Bourdieu, "Condition de classe et position de classe," 205–6. There is here, too, a direct influence of Friedrich Nietzsche's conception of "sense of power" in this conception of position and trajectory. For Nietzsche it was not merely the amount of power that explained how people behaved but rather their sense of power. If I have x amount of power and feel my power is declining, I might tend to deploy my power viciously and with venom. If I have the same x amount of power and feel that my power is increasing, I might be magnanimous and gentle. See Nietzsche, *Daybreak*.

33 Bourdieu, "Condition de classe et position de classe," 206.

34 Bourdieu, "The Future of Class and the Causality of the Probable," 242–43. Bourdieu uses the word *la pente*, which translates as "angle" but only to the extent of it being a measure of the steepness of the path ahead.

35 Bourdieu, *Distinction*, 194.

36 Bourdieu, *In Other Words*, 88.

37 Bourdieu, *Pascalian Meditations*, 140–41.

38 Heilbron, "Auguste Comte and the Second Scientific Revolution."

39 Comte, *Positive Philosophy*, 432.

40 Such a metaphoric conception plays a notable role in the literary imaginary of Milan Kundera in his well-known book, *The Unbearable Lightness of Being*, but even more so in *The Book of Laughter and Forgetting*, where forms of social gravity are consistently seen as behind the process of memory. See Kundera, *The Book of Laughter and Forgetting*; and Kundera, *The Unbearable Lightness of Being*.

41 Quetelet, "Recherches sur le penchant au crime aux différens âges," 4.

42 Carey, *Principles of Social Science*, 1:42, emphasis in the original.

43 See Hage, "A Not So Multi-Sited Ethnography."

44 Bourdieu, *The Field of Cultural Production*, 150–51, emphasis in the original.

45 Bourdieu, *The Field of Cultural Production*, 148–50.

46 Bourdieu, *The Field of Cultural Production*, 152–53.

47 Hage, *The Racial Politics of Australian Multiculturalism*, 216–18; Hage, *The Diasporic Condition*.

48 Bourdieu, *The Social Structures of the Economy*, 194.

Conclusion

1 As Bourdieu, *Language and Symbolic Power*, 242, makes clear, "The social world is, to a great extent, something which agents make at every moment."

2 Durkheim, *Textes*, 1:146.

3 Lacan, *Écrits*, 324, defines the real as "that which subsists outside of symbolization."

4 Héran, "La seconde nature de l'habitus," 388. A person who is socially *malade* is someone who is socially "sick" in the sense of not being able to deploy themselves well in the world. As the German neurologist and psychiatrist Kurt Goldstein, whom Bourdieu uses approvingly to analyze the practical inadequacy of the Algerian peasants as French capitalism imposes its reality on them, points out in "Health as Value," 183, "Health is not an objective condition which can be understood by the methods of natural science alone. . . . 'Health' appears thus as a value; its value consists in the individual's capacity to actualize his nature to the degree that, for him at least, it is essential. 'Being sick' appears as a loss or diminution of value, the value of self-realization, of existence."

5 I would have loved to include here a photo of the cartoon character Wile E. Coyote, pictured carrying on his back a snow-making "refrigerator" that manufactures the snow and projects it in front of him as he skis downhill, but because of copyright matters I am not allowed to do so. I urge those interested to find the image online.

6 Nordmann, *Bourdieu, Rancière*.

7 Rancière, *Disagreement*, 42.

8 Rancière, *Dissensus*, 38. Thanks to Greg Burris for alerting me to this passage.

9 Bourdieu, *Algerian Sketches*, 48; Bourdieu and Sayad, *Uprooting*, 123.

10 Bourdieu, *Travail et travailleurs en Algérie*, 201.

11 Bourdieu, "Social Space and Symbolic Power," 16–17.

12 Bourdieu, "Champ du pouvoir et division du travail de domination";
    Bourdieu and Saint Martin, *The State Nobility*, 261–339.

13 Bourdieu, *Masculine Domination*, 49–50.

14 This argument underlies the early work of Bourdieu and Jean-Claude
    Passeron on education. See Bourdieu and Passeron, *Reproduction in
    Education, Society and Culture*.

15 Hage, *The Racial Politics of Australian Multiculturalism*, 75–80.

16 Berlant, *Cruel Optimism*.

17 Bourdieu, *Sociologie générale*, 2:972.

18 Bourdieu, *The State Nobility*, 6.

19 For a description of the doxic character of the school calendar, see
    Bourdieu, *On the State*, 171–73. For a Durkheimian account of a chal-
    lenge to the Gregorian system, see Zerubavel, "The French Republican
    Calendar."

20 Bourdieu, *The Field of Cultural Production*, 83.

21 Bourdieu, *Pascalian Meditations*, 215.

22 Bourdieu, "The Royal Science and the Fatalism of Probability," 109.

23 Bourdieu, *On the State*, 3.

24 See, for example, Lahire, *The Plural Actor*, 145.

25 Bourdieu, *The Weight of the World*, 616.

26 Bourdieu, "Introduction à la socioanalyse"; Bourdieu, *The Weight of
    the World*, 611.

27 Bourdieu, *The Weight of the World*.

Bibliography

Aristotle. *Metaphysics: Book Theta*. Edited by Stephen Makin. Oxford: Oxford University Press, 2006.

Aristotle. *Metaphysics: Books Gamma, Delta, and Epsilon*. Edited by Christopher Kirwan. Oxford: Oxford University Press, 1993.

Austin, J. L. *Sense and Sensibilia*. Edited by Geoffrey James Warnock. London: Oxford University Press, 1962.

Bachelard, Gaston. *L'activité rationaliste de la physique contemporaine*. Paris: Presses Universitaires de France, 1977.

Beiser, Frederick C. *The German Historicist Tradition*. Oxford: Oxford University Press, 2011.

Bennett, Tony. *Habit's Pathways: Repetition, Power, Conduct*. Durham, NC: Duke University Press, 2023.

Berlant, Lauren. *Cruel Optimism*. Durham, NC: Duke University Press, 2011.

Bhaskar, Roy. *A Realist Theory of Science*. London: Routledge, 2008.

Bidet, Jacques. "Questions to Pierre Bourdieu." Translated by Anne Bailey. *Critique of Anthropology* 4, nos. 13–14 (1979): 203–8.

Boas, Franz. "Anthropology." In *Encyclopaedia of the Social Sciences*, edited by Edwin R. A. Seligman and Alvin Johnson, vol. 2, *Alliance–Brigandage*. New York: Macmillan, 1930.

Bolmain, Thomas. *Pierre Bourdieu philosophe: Une critique socio-philosophique de la "condition étudiante."* Namur, Belgium: Bibliothèque de Philosophie Sociale et Politique, 2017.

Bourdieu, Pierre. "Algerian Landing." Translated by Richard Nice and Loïc Wacquant. *Ethnography* 5, no. 4 (2004): 415–43.

Bourdieu, Pierre. *Algerian Sketches*. Edited by Tassadit Yacine. Translated by David Fernbach. Malden, MA: Polity, 2013.

Bourdieu, Pierre. "Annexe: Entretien de Pierre Bourdieu avec Gisèle Sapiro." Interview by Gisèle Sapiro. In *Pierre Bourdieu, sociologue*, edited by Louis Pinto, Gisèle Sapiro, and Patrick Champagne. Paris: Fayard, 2004.

Bourdieu, Pierre. *Anthropologie économique: Cours au Collège de France 1992–1993*. Paris: Seuil, 2017.

Bourdieu, Pierre. "Champ du pouvoir et division du travail de domination." *Actes de la Recherche en Sciences Sociales* 190 (2011): 126–39.

Bourdieu, Pierre. "Concluding Remarks: For a Sociogenetic Understanding of Intellectual Works." Translated by Nicole Kaplan, Craig Calhoun, and Leah Florence. In *Bourdieu: Critical Perspectives*, edited by
Craig Calhoun, Edward LiPuma, and Moishe Postone. Chicago: University of Chicago Press, 1993.

Bourdieu, Pierre. "Condition de classe et position de classe." *Archives Eu-
ropéen de Sociologie* 7, no. 2 (1966): 201–29.

Bourdieu, Pierre. *Distinction: A Social Critique of the Judgement of Taste.*
Translated by Richard Nice. Cambridge, MA: Harvard University
Press, 1984.

Bourdieu, Pierre. *The Field of Cultural Production: Essays on Art and Literature.* Edited by Randal Johnson. New York: Columbia University
Press, 1993.

Bourdieu, Pierre. "Forms of Capital." Translated by Richard Nice. In
Handbook of Theory and Research for the Sociology of Education, edited
by John G. Richardson. New York: Greenwood, 1986.

Bourdieu, Pierre. "From Ruling Class to Field of Power: An Interview with
Pierre Bourdieu on La Noblesse d'État." Interview by Loïc J. D. Wacquant. Translated by Loïc J. D. Wacquant. *Theory, Culture and Society*
10, no. 3 (1993): 19–44.

Bourdieu, Pierre. "The Future of Class and the Causality of the Probable."
Translated by Michael Grenfell. In *Re-Thinking Economics: Exploring
the Work of Pierre Bourdieu*, edited by Asimina Christoforou and Michael Lainé. New York: Routledge, 2014.

Bourdieu, Pierre. *General Sociology.* Vol. 1, *Classification Struggles: Lectures
at the Collège de France 1981–1982*. Edited by Patrick Champagne, Julien
Duval, Franck Poupeau, and Marie-Christine Rivière. Translated by
Peter Collier. Cambridge: Polity, 2018.

Bourdieu, Pierre. *In Other Words: Essays Towards a Reflexive Sociology.*
Translated by Matthew Adamson. Stanford, CA: Stanford University
Press, 1990.

Bourdieu, Pierre. "Intellectual Field and Creative Project." Translated by
Sian France. *Social Science Information* 8, no. 2 (1969): 89–119.

Bourdieu, Pierre. "Intellectuals and the Internationalization of Ideas: An Interview with M'Hammed Sabour." Translated by M'Hammed Sabour.
International Journal of Contemporary Sociology 33, no. 2 (1996): 237–53.

Bourdieu, Pierre. "Introduction à la socioanalyse." *Actes de la Recherche en
Sciences Sociales* 90 (1991): 3–5.

Bourdieu, Pierre. "The Invention of the Artist's Life." Translated by
Erec R. Koch. *Yale French Studies* 73 (1987): 75–103.

Bourdieu, Pierre. "La dernière instance." In *La siècle de Kafka*, edited by Yasha David. Paris: Centre Georges Pompidou, 1984.

Bourdieu, Pierre. *Language and Symbolic Power.* Edited by John B. Thompson. Translated by Gino Raymond and Matthew Adamson. Cambridge: Polity, 1991.

Bourdieu, Pierre. "Les trois états du capital culturel." *Actes de la Recherche en Sciences Sociales* 30 (1979): 3–6.

Bourdieu, Pierre. *The Logic of Practice.* Translated by Richard Nice. Cambridge: Polity, 1990.

Bourdieu, Pierre. *Masculine Domination.* Translated by Richard Nice. Cambridge: Polity, 2001.

Bourdieu, Pierre. "Men and Machines." In *Advances in Social Theory and Methodology: Toward an Integration of Micro- and Macro-Sociologies,* edited by K. Knorr-Cetina and A. V. Cicourel. Boston: Routledge and Kegan Paul, 1981.

Bourdieu, Pierre. *Microcosmes: Théorie de champs.* Paris: Éditions Raisons d'Agir, 2022.

Bourdieu, Pierre. *On the State: Lectures at the Collège de France 1989–1992.* Edited by Patrick Champagne, Remy Lenoir, Frank Poupeau, and Marie-Christine Rivière. Translated by David Fernbach. Cambridge: Polity, 2014.

Bourdieu, Pierre. "Outline of a Sociological Theory of Art Perception." *International Social Science Journal* 20 (1968): 589–612.

Bourdieu, Pierre. *Outline of a Theory of Practice.* Translated by Richard Nice. Cambridge: Cambridge University Press, 1977.

Bourdieu, Pierre. *Pascalian Meditations.* Translated by Richard Nice. Stanford, CA: Stanford University Press, 2000.

Bourdieu, Pierre. "The Philosophical Institution." Translated by Kathleen McLaughlin. In *Philosophy in France Today,* edited by Alan Montefiore. Cambridge: Cambridge University Press, 1983.

Bourdieu, Pierre. *Political Interventions: Social Science and Political Action.* Translated by David Fernbach. London: Verso, 2008.

Bourdieu, Pierre. *The Political Ontology of Martin Heidegger.* Translated by Peter Collier. Oxford: Polity, 1991.

Bourdieu, Pierre. *Practical Reason: On the Theory of Action.* Cambridge: Polity, 1998.

Bourdieu, Pierre. "Préface." In *Les chômeurs de Marienthal,* by Paul F. Lazarsfeld, Marie Jahoda, and Hans Zeisel. Paris: Éditions de Minuit, 1981.

Bourdieu, Pierre. *Retour sur la réflexivité.* Edited by Jérôme Bourdieu and Johan Heilbron. Paris: Éditions de l'EHESS, 2022.

Bourdieu, Pierre. "The Royal Science and the Fatalism of Probability." In *Political Interventions*, edited by Franck Poupeau and Thierry Discepolo. Translated by David Fernbach. London: Verso, 2008.

Bourdieu, Pierre. *The Rules of Art: Genesis and Structure of the Literary Field*. Translated by Susan Emanuel. Cambridge: Polity, 1996.

Bourdieu, Pierre. "Scattered Remarks." Translated by Tarik Wareh and Loïc J. D. Wacquant. *European Journal of Social Theory* 2, no. 3 (1999): 334–40.

Bourdieu, Pierre. "The Scholastic Point of View." Translated by Loïc J. D. Wacquant. *Cultural Anthropology* 5, no. 4 (1990): 380–91.

Bourdieu, Pierre. *Sketch for a Self-Analysis*. Translated by Richard Nice. Cambridge: Polity, 2007.

Bourdieu, Pierre. "Social Space and Symbolic Power." Translated by Loïc J. D. Wacquant. *Sociological Theory* 7, no. 1 (1989): 14–25.

Bourdieu, Pierre. *The Social Structures of the Economy*. Translated by Chris Turner. Cambridge: Polity, 2005.

Bourdieu, Pierre. *Sociologie générale*. Vol. 1, *Habitus—champ: Cours au Collège de France 1981–1983*. Paris: Seuil, 2015.

Bourdieu, Pierre. *Sociologie générale*. Vol. 2, *Capital: Cours au Collège de France 1983–1986*. Paris: Seuil, 2016.

Bourdieu, Pierre. "Sociologists of Beliefs and Beliefs of Sociologists." Translated by Véronique Altglas and Matthew Wood. *Nordic Journal of Religion and Society* 23, no. 1 (2010): 1–7.

Bourdieu, Pierre. *Sociology in Question*. Translated by Richard Nice. London: Sage, 1993.

Bourdieu, Pierre. "Structuralism and Theory of Sociological Knowledge." Translated by Angela Zanotti-Karp. *Social Research* 35, no. 4 (1968): 681–706.

Bourdieu, Pierre. "Symbolic Capital and Social Classes." Translated by Loïc Wacquant. *Journal of Classical Sociology* 13, no. 2 (2013): 292–302.

Bourdieu, Pierre. *Travail et travailleurs en Algérie*. Rev. ed. Edited by Amín Pérez and Tassadit Yacine. Paris: Éditions Raisons d'Agir, 2021.

Bourdieu, Pierre. "What Makes a Social Class?" Translated by Loïc J. D. Wacquant and David Young. *Berkeley Journal of Sociology* 22 (1987): 1–18.

Bourdieu, Pierre, Alain Accardo, Gabrielle Balazs, et al. *La misère du monde*. Paris: Seuil, 1993.

Bourdieu, Pierre, Alain Accardo, Gabrielle Balazs, et al. *The Weight of the World: Social Suffering in Contemporary Society*. Translated by Priscilla Parkhurst Ferguson, Susan Emanuel, Joe Johnson, and Shoggy T. Waryn. Stanford, CA: Stanford University Press, 1999.

Bourdieu, Pierre, and Roger Chartier. "Gens à histoire, gens sans histoire: Dialogue entre Bourdieu et Chartier." *Politix* 2, no. 6 (1989): 53–60.

Bourdieu, Pierre, and Yvette Delsaut. "Le couturier et sa griffe: Contribution à une théorie de la magie." *Actes de la Recherche en Sciences Sociales* 1, no. 1 (1975): 7–36.

Bourdieu, Pierre, and Yvette Delsaut. "Pour un sociologie de la perception." *Actes de la Recherche en Sciences Sociales* 40 (1981): 3–9.

Bourdieu, Pierre, and Jean-Claude Passeron. *Reproduction in Education, Society and Culture.* Translated by Richard Nice. London: Sage, 1977.

Bourdieu, Pierre, with Monique de Saint Martin. *The State Nobility: Elite Schools in the Field of Power.* Translated by Loretta C. Clough. Cambridge: Polity, 1996.

Bourdieu, Pierre, and Abdelmalek Sayad. *Uprooting: The Crisis of Traditional Agriculture in Algeria.* Edited by Paul A. Silverstein. Translated by Susan Emanuel. Cambridge: Polity, 2020.

Bourdieu, Pierre, and Loïc J. D. Wacquant. *An Invitation to Reflexive Sociology.* Chicago: University of Chicago Press, 1992.

Braz, Adelino. *Bourdieu.* Paris: Ellipses, 2017.

Butler, Judith. *Excitable Speech: A Politics of the Performative.* New York: Routledge, 1997.

Calhoun, Craig. "Habitus, Field, and Capital: The Question of Historical Specificity." In *Bourdieu: Critical Perspectives,* edited by Craig Calhoun, Edward LiPuma, and Moishe Postone. Chicago: University of Chicago Press, 1993.

Camic, Charles. "The Matter of Habit." *American Journal of Sociology* 91, no. 5 (1986): 1039–87.

Carey, Henry C. *Principles of Social Science.* Vol. 1. Philadelphia: J. B. Lippincott, 1858.

Carlisle, Clare. *On Habit.* New York: Routledge, 2014.

Cassin, Barbara, Sandra Laugier, Alain de Libera, Irène Rosier-Catach, and Giacinta Spinosa. "Sense/Meaning." In *Dictionary of Untranslatables: A Philosophical Lexicon,* edited by Barbara Cassin, Emily S. Apter, Jacques Lezra, and Michael Wood. Princeton, NJ: Princeton University Press, 2014.

Chevallier, Stéphane, and Christiane Chauviré. *Dictionnaire Bourdieu.* Paris: Ellipses, 2010.

Comte, Auguste. *The Positive Philosophy of Auguste Comte.* Translated by Harriet Martineau. New York: Calvin Blanchard, 1855.

Connell, R. W. "The Black Box of Habit on the Wings of History: Critical Reflections on the Theory of Social Reproduction." In *Which Way Is Up? Essays on Class, Sex and Culture.* Sydney: George Allen and Unwin, 1983.

Deleuze, Gilles. *Difference and Repetition*. Translated by Paul Patton. New York: Columbia University Press, 1994.

Desan, Mathieu. "Bourdieu, Marx, and Capital: A Critique of the Extension Model." *Sociological Theory* 31, no. 4 (2013): 318–42.

Dreyfus, Hubert, and Paul Rabinow. "Can There Be a Science of Existential Structure and Social Meaning?" In *Bourdieu: Critical Perspectives*, edited by Craig Calhoun, Edward LiPuma, and Moishe Postone. Chicago: University of Chicago Press, 1993.

Dreyfus, Hubert L. *Being-in-the-World: A Commentary on Heidegger's "Being and Time," Division I*. Cambridge, MA: MIT Press, 1991.

Dubois, Jacques. "Flaubert analyste de Bourdieu." In *Bourdieu et la littérature*, edited by Jean-Pierre Martin. Nantes, France: Éditions Cécile Defaut, 2010.

Durkheim, Émile. "The Dualism of Human Nature and Its Social Conditions." Translated by Irène Eulriet and William Watts Miller. *Durkheimian Studies / Études Durkheimiennes* 11 (2005): 35–45.

Durkheim, Émile. *The Rules of Sociological Method*. Edited by Steven Lukes. Translated by W. D. Halls. New York: Free Press, 1982.

Durkheim, Émile. *Textes*. Vol. 1, *Éléments d'une théorie sociale*. Edited by Victor Karady. Paris: Éditions de Minuit, 1975.

Emirbayer, Mustafa. "Tilly and Bourdieu." *American Sociologist* 41, no. 4 (2010): 400–422.

Fanon, Frantz. *Black Skin, White Masks*. London: Pluto, 1986.

Foucault, Michel. *The Order of Things: An Archaeology of the Human Sciences*. London: Routledge, 2007.

Freud, Sigmund. "Instincts and Their Vicissitudes." In *The Standard Edition of the Complete Psychological Works of Sigmund Freud*, vol. 14, *1914–1916: On the History of the Psycho-Analytic Movement, Papers on Metapsychology, and Other Works*. Translated by James Strachey. London: Hogarth, 1957.

Freud, Sigmund. "The Sexual Theories of Children." In *The Standard Edition of the Complete Psychological Works of Sigmund Freud*, vol. 9, *1906–1908: Jensen's "Gradiva" and Other Works*. Translated by James Strachey. London: Hogarth, 1959.

Gautier, Claude. *La force du social. Enquête philosophique sur la sociologie des pratiques de Pierre Bourdieu*. Paris: Cerf, 2012.

Godelier, Maurice. "System, Structure and Contradiction in Capital." Translated by Ben Brewster. *Socialist Register* 4 (1967): 91–119.

Goldstein, Kurt. "Health as Value." In *Knowledge in Human Values*, edited by Abraham H. Maslow. New York: Harper, 1959.

Gorski, Philip S., ed. *Bourdieu and Historical Analysis*. Durham, NC: Duke University Press, 2013.

Hacking, Ian. *The Emergence of Probability: A Philosophical Study of Early Ideas About Probability, Induction and Statistical Inference.* London: Cambridge University Press, 1975.

Hacking, Ian. "Science de la science chez Pierre Bourdieu." In *La liberté par la connaissance: Pierre Bourdieu (1930–2002)*, edited by Jacques Bouveresse and Daniel Roche. Paris: Odile Jacob, 2004.

Hage, Ghassan. "Bearable Life." *Suomen Antropologi* 44, no. 2 (2019): 81–83.

Hage, Ghassan. "Decay as Decline in Social Viability Among Ex-Militiamen in Lebanon." In *Decay*, edited by Ghassan Hage. Durham, NC: Duke University Press, 2021.

Hage, Ghassan. *The Diasporic Condition: Ethnographic Explorations of the Lebanese in the World.* Chicago: University of Chicago Press, 2021.

Hage, Ghassan. "A Not So Multi-Sited Ethnography of a Not So Imagined Community." *Anthropological Theory* 5, no. 4 (2005): 463–75.

Hage, Ghassan. "Pierre Bourdieu in the Nineties: Between the Church and the Atelier." *Theory and Society* 23, no. 3 (1994): 419–40.

Hage, Ghassan. *The Racial Politics of Australian Multiculturalism: White Nation, Against Paranoid Nationalism and Later Writings.* Parramatta, New South Wales: Sweatshop Literacy Movement, 2023.

Halewood, Michael. "'Class Is Always a Matter of Morals': Bourdieu and Dewey on Social Class, Morality, and Habit(us)." *Cultural Sociology* 17, no. 3 (2023): 373–89.

Hegel, Georg Wilhelm Friedrich. *Hegel's Phenomenology of Spirit.* Translated by A. V. Miller. Oxford: Oxford University Press, 1977.

Heidegger, Martin. *Being and Time.* Translated by John Macquarrie and Edward Robinson. Oxford: Blackwell, 1962.

Heidegger, Martin. "Building Dwelling Thinking." In *Basic Writings*, edited by David Farrell Krell. Translated by Albert Hofstadter. New York: HarperCollins, 1993.

Heilbron, Johan. "Auguste Comte and the Second Scientific Revolution." In *The Anthem Companion to Auguste Comte*, edited by Andrew Wernick. London: Anthem, 2017.

Heilbron, Johan. *French Sociology.* Ithaca, NY: Cornell University Press, 2015.

Héran, François. "La seconde nature de l'habitus: Tradition philosophique et sens commun dans le langage sociologique." *Revue Française de Sociologie* 28, no. 3 (1987): 385–416.

Hilgers, Mathieu, and Éric Mangez, eds. *Bourdieu's Theory of Social Fields: Concepts and Applications.* New York: Routledge, 2015.

Huizinga, Johan. *Homo Ludens: A Study of the Play-Element in Culture.* London: Routledge and Kegan Paul, 1949.

Husserl, Edmund. *Ideas Pertaining to a Pure Phenomenology and to a Phenomenological Philosophy.* Vol. 2, *Studies in the Phenomenology of*

Constitution. Translated by Richard Rojcewicz and André Schuwer. Dordrecht, Netherlands: Kluwer Academic, 1989.

Husserl, Edmund. *Phenomenology and the Crisis of Philosophy.* Translated by Quentin Lauer. New York: Harper and Row, 1965.

Husserl, Edmund. *Zur Phänomenologie der Intersubjektivität: Textes aus dem Nachlass,* vol. 2, *1921–1928.* Edited by Iso Kern. The Hague, Netherlands: Martinus Nijhoff, 1973.

James, William. "The Gospel of Relaxation." In *The Heart of William James,* edited by Robert Dale Richardson. Cambridge, MA: Harvard University Press, 2012.

James, William. *Habit.* New York: Henry Holt, 1914.

Jung, C. G. "Psychoanalysis and Neurosis." In *The Collected Works of C. G. Jung,* vol. 4, *Freud and Psychoanalysis,* edited and translated by Gerhard Adler and R. F. C. Hull. Princeton, NJ: Princeton University Press, 1961.

Kojève, Alexandre. *Introduction to the Reading of Hegel.* Translated by James H. Nichols, Jr. New York: Basic Books, 1969.

Kristeva, Julia. *Revolution in Poetic Language.* Translated by Margaret Waller. New York: Columbia University Press, 1984.

Kundera, Milan. *The Book of Laughter and Forgetting.* Translated by Michael Henry Heim. New York: Alfred A. Knopf, 1980.

Kundera, Milan. *The Unbearable Lightness of Being.* Translated by Michael Henry Heim. New York: Harper and Row, 1984.

Lacan, Jacques. *Écrits: The First Complete Edition in English.* Translated by Bruce Fink. New York: W. W. Norton, 2005.

Lacan, Jacques. *The Seminar of Jacques Lacan.* Vol. 3, *The Psychoses 1955–1956.* Edited by Jacques-Alain Miller. Translated by Russell Grigg. Hove, UK: Routledge, 2013.

Lacan, Jacques. "The Signification of the Phallus." In *Ecrits: The First Complete Edition in English,* translated by Bruce Fink. New York: W. W. Norton, 2005.

Lahire, Bernard. *The Plural Actor.* Translated by David Fernbach. Cambridge: Polity, 2011.

Lamont, Michèle. *Money, Morals, and Manners: The Culture of the French and the American Upper-Middle Class.* Chicago: University of Chicago Press, 1992.

Latour, Bruno. *An Inquiry into Modes of Existence: An Anthropology of the Moderns.* Translated by Catherine Porter. Cambridge, MA: Harvard University Press, 2013.

Lentacker, Antoine. *La science des institutions impures. Bourdieu critique de Lévi-Strauss,* "Cours & Travaux." Paris: Raisons d'agir, 2010.

Lescourret, Marie-Anne. "Pierre Bourdieu: Un philosophe en sociologie." In *Pierre Bourdieu: Un philosophe en sociologie*, edited by Marie-Anne Lescourret. Paris: Presses Universitaires de France, 2009.

Lévi-Strauss, Claude, and Didier Eribon. *Conversations with Claude Lévi-Strauss*. Translated by Paula Wissing. Chicago: University of Chicago Press, 1991.

Maître, Jacques, and Pierre Bourdieu. "Avant-propos dialogué." In *L'autobiographie d'un paranoïaque: L'abbé Berry (1878–1947) et le roman de Billy Introïbo*. Paris: Anthropos, 1994.

Malabou, Catherine. *What Should We Do with Our Brain?* Translated by Sebastian Rand. New York: Fordham University Press, 2008.

Marx, Karl. *Capital: A Critique of Political Economy*. Vol. 1. Edited by Paul North and Paul Reitter. Translated by Paul Reitter. Princeton, NJ: Princeton University Press, 2024.

Mauss, Marcel. *The Gift: The Form and Reason for Exchange in Archaic Societies*. Translated by W. D. Halls. Abingdon, UK: Routledge, 2004.

Mead, Geoffrey. "Bourdieu and Conscious Deliberation: An Anti-Mechanistic Solution." *European Journal of Social Theory* 19, no. 1 (2016): 57–73.

Mead, Geoffrey. "Forms of Knowledge and the Love of Necessity in Bourdieu's Clinical Sociology." *Sociological Review* 65, no. 4 (2017): 628–43.

Merleau-Ponty, Maurice. *Phenomenology of Perception*. Translated by Donald A. Landes. Abingdon, UK: Routledge, 2012.

Merleau-Ponty, Maurice. *The Structure of Behavior*. Translated by Alden L. Fisher. Boston: Beacon, 1963.

Meyer, Michel. "Présentation." *Revue Internationale de Philosophie* 56, no. 220 (2002): 177–78.

Nadler, Steven M. *Think Least of Death: Spinoza on How to Live and How to Die*. Princeton, NJ: Princeton University Press, 2020.

Nietzsche, Friedrich. *Daybreak: Thoughts on the Prejudices of Morality*. Edited by Maudemarie Clark and Brian Leiter. Translated by R. J. Hollingdale. Cambridge: Cambridge University Press, 1997.

Nietzsche, Friedrich. *On the Genealogy of Morals*. Edited by Walter Kaufmann. Translated by Walter Kaufmann and R. J. Hollingdale. New York: Vintage Books, 1989.

Nordmann, Charlotte. *Bourdieu, Rancière: La politique entre sociologie et philosophie*. Paris: Éditions Amsterdam, 2007.

Pascal, Blaise. *Pensées and Other Writings*. Edited by Anthony Levi. Translated by Honor Levi. Oxford: Oxford University Press, 1995.

Pérez, Amín. *Bourdieu and Sayad Against Empire: Forging Sociology in Anticolonial Struggle*. Translated by Andrew Brown. Cambridge: Polity, 2024.

Perreau, Laurent. *Bourdieu et la phénoménologie: Théorie du sujet social*. Paris: CNRS Éditions, 2019.

Perreau, Laurent. "'Quelque chose comme un sujet': Bourdieu et la phénoménologie sociale." In *Bourdieu: Théoricien de la pratique*, edited by Michel de Fornel and Albert Ogien. Paris: Éditions de l'EHESS, 2011.

"Pierre Bourdieu et la philosophie," special issue, *Revue Internationale de Philosophie* 56, no. 220 (2002).

Pinto, Louis. "Pierre Bourdieu et la sociologie d'Émile Durkheim." In *Lectures de Bourdieu*, edited by Frédéric Lebaron and Gerard Mauger, 61–74. Paris: Ellipses, 2012.

Pinto, Louis. *Pierre Bourdieu et la théorie du monde social*. Paris: A. Michel, 1998.

Plato. *Theaetetus and Sophist*. Edited and translated by Christopher Rowe. Cambridge Texts in the History of Philosophy. Cambridge: Cambridge University Press, 2015.

Quetelet, Adolphe. "Recherches sur le penchant au crime aux différens âges." *Mémoires de l'Académie Royale de Belgique* 7 (1832): 1–87.

Rancière, Jacques. *Disagreement: Politics and Philosophy*. Translated by Julie Rose. Minneapolis: University of Minnesota Press, 1999.

Rancière, Jacques. *Dissensus: On Politics and Aesthetics*. Edited and translated by Steven Corcoran. London: Continuum, 2010.

Rey, Jean-François. "Faire le temps: D'une phénoménologie des attitudes temporelles à une théorie des pratiques temporelles." In *Pierre Bourdieu: Un philosophe en sociologie*, edited by Marie-Anne Lescourret. Paris: Presses Universitaires de France, 2009.

Rodrigo, Pierre. "The Dynamic of *Hexis* in Aristotle's Philosophy." Translated by Clare Carlisle. *Journal of the British Society for Phenomenology* 42, no. 1 (2011): 6–17.

Rolland de Renéville, Jacques. *Itinéraire du sens*. Paris: Presses Universitaires de France, 1982.

Sartre, Jean-Paul. *Being and Nothingness: An Essay in Phenomenological Ontology*. Translated by Sarah Richmond. Abingdon, UK: Routledge, 2020.

Sartre, Jean-Paul. *Existentialism Is a Humanism*. Translated by Carol Macomber. New Haven, CT: Yale University Press, 2007.

Saussure, Ferdinand de. *Course in General Linguistics*. Translated by Roy Harris. London: Bloomsbury, 2013.

Shusterman, Richard. "Bourdieu as Philosopher." In *Bourdieu: A Critical Reader*, edited by Richard Shusterman. Malden, MA: Blackwell, 1999.

Silva, Elizabeth B. "Unity and Fragmentation of the Habitus." *Sociological Review* 64, no. 1 (2016): 166–83.

Sparrow, Tom, and Adam Hutchinson, eds. *A History of Habit: From Aristotle to Bourdieu.* Lanham, MD: Lexington Books, 2015.

Spinoza, Benedictus de. *The Collected Works of Spinoza.* Vol. 1. Edited and translated by Edwin Curley. Princeton, NJ: Princeton University Press, 1985.

Steinmetz, George. "Bourdieu's Disavowal of Lacan: Psychoanalytic Theory and the Concepts of 'Habitus' and 'Symbolic Capital.'" *Constellations* 13, no. 4 (2006): 445–64.

Steinmetz, George. "Social Fields, Subfields and Social Spaces at the Scale of Empires: Explaining the Colonial State and Colonial Sociology." *Sociological Review Monographs* 64, no. 2 (2016): 98–123.

Swartz, David L. *Culture and Power: The Sociology of Pierre Bourdieu.* Chicago: University of Chicago Press, 1997.

Swartz, David L. *Symbolic Power, Politics, and Intellectuals: The Political Sociology of Pierre Bourdieu.* Chicago: University of Chicago Press, 2013.

Threadgold, Steven. *Bourdieu and Affect: Towards a Theory of Affective Affinities.* Bristol, UK: Bristol University Press, 2020.

Tokarczuk, Olga. *Drive Your Plow over the Bones of the Dead.* Translated by Antonia Lloyd-Jones. New York: Riverhead Books, 2019.

Tylor, Edward Burnett. *Primitive Culture: Researches into the Development of Mythology, Philosophy, Religion, Art, and Custom.* London: John Murray, 1891.

Vandenberghe, Frédéric. "'The Real Is Relational': An Epistemological Analysis of Pierre Bourdieu's Generative Structuralism." *Sociological Theory* 17, no. 1 (1999): 32–67.

Viveiros de Castro, Eduardo. *Cannibal Metaphysics: For a Post-Structural Anthropology.* Edited and translated by Peter Skafish. Minneapolis: Univocal, 2014.

Wacquant, Loïc. "A Concise Genealogy and Anatomy of Habitus." *Sociological Review* 64, no. 1 (2016): 64–72.

Wacquant, Loïc J. D. "Durkheim and Bourdieu: The Common Plinth and Its Cracks." In *Reading Bourdieu on Society and Culture*, edited by Bridget Fowler. Translated by Tarik Wareh. Oxford: Blackwell, 2000.

Weber, Max. *Economy and Society: An Outline of Interpretive Sociology.* Edited by Guenther Roth and Claus Wittich. Translated by Ephraim Fischoff, Hans Gerth, A. M. Henderson, et al. Berkeley: University of California Press, 1978.

Wittgenstein, Ludwig. *Philosophical Investigations*. Rev. 4th ed. Edited by P. M. S. Hacker and Joachim Schulte. Translated by G. E. M. Anscombe, P. M. S. Hacker, and Joachim Schulte. Chichester, UK: John Wiley and Sons, 2010.

Zerubavel, Eviatar. "The French Republican Calendar: A Case Study in the Sociology of Time." *American Sociological Review* 42, no. 6 (1977): 868–77.

Index

actor, avoiding concept of, 21–22
agents. *See* social agents
Althusser, Louis, 22, 116
analytical concept: field as, 93–96;
   illusio as, 71–75
Aquinas, Thomas, 44
aristocratic domination, 121–23
augmentation, term, 1–2, 5
Austin, J. L., 8
Australia, assimilation in, 125
Australian male, identifying, 81
avoidance, form of, 25

Bachelard, Gaston, 10, 101
being: deafness and, 59–61; practical
   being, 24–26; reflexivity and lucidity, 131–32
Beirut-Rafic Hariri International Airport, 111–12
Bennett, Tony, 30
Bhaskar, Roy, 47
Biden, Joe, 129
Bildung, 83
Boas, Franz, 28
body knowledge, highlighting, 34
Bourdieu, Pierre, 1; birth of perspectivism of, 10–11; conceptualization of practice, 103; and existential
   ecologies, 113–32; following the
   Durkheimian lineage, 3; and habituation correlation, 41–61; means and
   ends of recognition, 80–91; and
   philosophy, 6–8; and problematic of
   scholastic view, 8–11; production/
   distribution of meaningful life, 62–79;
   seeing social world as economy,
   66–67; and social aging, 77; social
   complicity/efficiency, 20–40; social physics of existential mobility,

92–112; on strategy, 58–59; taking
   perspectivism seriously, 11–19; talking of "social being," 3–4; transforming conception of centrality of
   play, 64–65; views on dispositionality, 50; writing as mode for public
   intervention, 43–44
Bourdieusian/Durkheimian differentiation, 29–30
building-dwelling relation, 68
"Building Dwelling Thinking"
   (Heidegger), 68
Butler, Judith, 36

Calhoun, Craig, 81
Canguilhem, Georges, 6, 10, 24
capacity: concerning socially constructed realities, 57–59; eavesdropping dispositions, 51; generative
   mechanism, 46–51; habitus as theory
   of what we are, 44–46; habitus
   between reproduction and social
   change, 41–44; hearing capacities, 51
capital, 1, 3, 5–6, 15, 17–18, 20, 42, 70;
   as accumulated labor, 83; accumulation of, 18, 106; affinity with
   economic logic, 82; amounts of, 82;
   cultural capital, 20, 80, 83–85, 121;
   deploying as analytic category, 82;
   distribution of, 98, 100; forms of,
   18, 81, 83, 85, 97, 101; between habitus and *illusio*, 83–85; and *illusio* as
   analytic category, 71–75; originality
   of conceptions of, 80–81; as possession, 85–87; as recognition, 85–87;
   recognition as distinction and legitimacy, 88–91; and social gravity,
   107–10; socioexistential physics of
   fields, 103–7; species of, 83; as stake

www.ingramcontent.com/pod-product-compliance
Lightning Source LLC
Chambersburg PA
CBHW020543270326
41927CB00006B/695

9 781478 032625